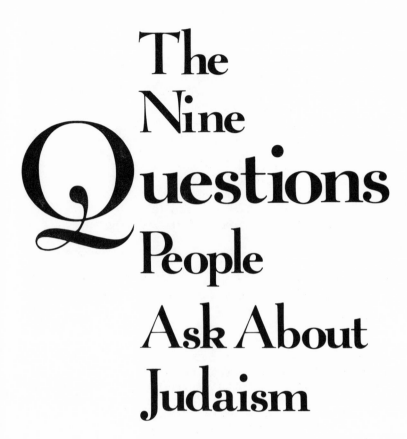

The Nine Questions People Ask About Judaism

by
*DENNIS PRAGER and
JOSEPH TELUSHKIN*

Foreword by Herman Wouk

Simon and Schuster   *New York*

Published by Simon and Schuster
A Division of Gulf & Western Corporation
Simon & Schuster Building
Rockefeller Center
1230 Avenue of the Americas
New York, New York 10020
SIMON AND SCHUSTER and colophon are
trademarks of Simon & Schuster
Designed by Irving Perkins and Associates
Manufactured in the United States of America

10 9 8 7 6 5 4 3 2 1

Library of Congress Cataloging in
Publication Data

Prager, Dennis, date
    The nine questions people ask about Judaism.
    Previously published as: Eight questions
people ask about Judaism. 1975.
    Includes bibliographical references.
    1. Orthodox Judaism—Addresses, essays,
lectures. 2. Jewish way of life—Addresses, essays,
lectures. I. Telushkin, Joseph, date. II. Title.
BM565.P7   1981   296.7'4   81-5694
                                        AACR2
ISBN 0-671-42593-5

A previous edition of this book
was published under the title
Eight Questions People Ask About Judaism.

Acknowledgments

An earlier edition of this book was printed in 1975 under the title *Eight Questions People Ask About Judaism*. In that edition we noted with gratitude the names of certain individuals with whom we had had particularly rewarding discussions about Judaism or whose writings had especially influenced us. They were Dr. Shlomo Bardin and Rabbis Eliezer Berkovits, Saul Berman, David Eliach, Norman Frimer, Irving Greenberg, Robert Hirt, Steven Riskin, and Avraham Weiss. In addition, we thanked Dr. Howard Siegel, Shalva Siegel, Dr. Steven M. Cohen, Jerry Unterman, and Jon Groner for their insightful suggestions, criticisms, and stylistic advice.

With regard to *The Nine Questions People Ask About Judaism*, we are particularly grateful to our close friends Michael and Nancy Medved for all their assistance and for bringing *Eight Questions* to the attention of the publisher; to Fred Hills, our demanding but constantly supportive editor; to Veronica Johnson for her extraordinary copy editing; and to Corrine Winner who was of such great assistance in preparing the manuscript.

For our parents,
Max and Hilda Prager
and
Shlomo and Helen Telushkin,
who provided environments conducive
to asking questions and seeking
answers

Contents

10

Foreword

Dear Joe and Dennis,

My son Joe brought home a set of galleys of *The Nine Questions People Ask About Judaism*. I congratulate you both. It's a creative, energetic, hard-headed book. I'm personally moved and encouraged by it.

My original title for *This Is My God* was *The Intelligent Skeptic's Guide to Judaism*. But I discerned that my book in essence was a personal statement, not an effort to take on hard recurring questions and convince other people with my answers. We work in different ways. *This Is My God* in draft contained argumentative passages that weren't bad, but I focused and completed the work as one man's statement of faith.

Now you have actually written *The Intelligent Skeptic's Guide to Judaism*. Your material specifically moves in the tough mental universe of collegians and post-collegians. . . . The book should do a lot of good.

My son has told me something of how you came to evolve this book; I mean the lectures on campuses, the rather shocking reactions of some teenagers, your experiences in the Soviet Union, and so forth. I am glad that you have incorporated some personal views into your introductory essays, which give us a better sense of the voices we hear on the pages that follow. Now I can understand how, in trying to teach Judaism in the setting of the '70s and '80s, the objections you encountered have tended to coalesce into these nine, which in sum reflect the old challenge, taking the special color of contemporary times.

The best of luck with this very fine book.

HERMAN WOUK

Preface

People often ask me why I returned to Judaism. "I saw the rest of the world," I tell them.

This answer is meant neither to denigrate other cultures or religions nor to be flippant. But the more I come to know and experience the world and its history, the more I come to venerate Judaism and the nation which it has produced.

I remember walking around the exquisite Indonesian island of Bali, seeing men gathered everywhere cheering at cock fights. Watching animals scratch each other's eyes out was as entertaining to these men as a baseball game was to me—and as morally unproblematic.

Which brings me to the heart of the issue. From an early age I have been obsessed by issues of good and evil. Why is the world and its history so filled with cruelty? Why do people intentionally hurt other people? Are all evil people sick, and if not (as I am now convinced), should we not be preoccupied with one question: How can we make better, kinder, finer human beings?

From my teens until today, the significance of all other questions has paled in comparison. As a result, all my life I have been searching—not for Truth or Happiness nor The Way nor The Light. Not even, at least not consciously, for God. All I have ever wanted to know is whether there exists a way of life—religious or secular, Eastern or Western, rational or mystical—which is likely, or at least the most likely, to unlock whatever goodness lies in human beings.

13

This search has taken me alone through sixty countries and to experiences as far from my religious Jewish upbringing as can be imagined.

My search has brought me to Judaism. I believe it offers the best answers to the terrible problem of how to achieve goodness among a race of beings not strongly predisposed to its achievement. If I were not convinced of this, I would not actively identify with, let alone advocate, Judaism. After the Holocaust, and in an open society, one needs powerful reasons to be a Jew.

I offer some of these reasons in this book, written with Joseph Telushkin, who has been my beloved friend since our second year in high school, and with whom I have shared every idea and struggle. It is very reassuring to note, however, that our ideas are not new. We are only attempting to restate for our generation what Isaiah and others stated for all generations.

"The Jewish people," said Abraham Joshua Heschel, in what I believe is the single most accurate description of Jews today, "is a messenger who forgot his message." Here is that message as two products of Judaism and Western reason see it.

—DENNIS PRAGER

Years ago, while being served a kosher meal on a plane flight, Dennis Prager asked the stewardess if she knew the meaning of kosher. "Food blessed by a rabbi," she responded. Intrigued by this unique interpretation, I asked the same question of a stewardess the next time I flew, and I received the same response. She then asked me, "If a rabbi blesses pig, does the pig become kosher?" Glibly I responded, "No, but the rabbi becomes unkosher." She told me that she knew about Kashrut from her Jewish ex-boyfriend.

I was in a glum mood the rest of the flight. The laws of Kashrut had regulated for thousands of years that an animal be killed as quickly and painlessly as possible, that Jews not eat any animal they wanted, and that Jews not hunt. Now, Kashrut, and Judaism in general, with this three-thousand-year tradition of ethical striving, was being turned into voodoo rites. People believed that somewhere in the United States chickens were marching past rabbis who blessed them "kosher."

My unhappiness was intensified because Judaism has been the passion of my life. At the age of six, I entered a Jewish day school where Hebrew and Judaism were studied four hours a day. Since my teens, I have studied Jewish law, Jewish theology, and Jewish history intensively. One source of this passion for Judaism is my grandfather, Rabbi Nissen Telushkin, of blessed memory. Among my most powerful memories is the kiss he bestowed on my head a few months before he died, when I told him that I had decided to study for the rabbinate. He had been a rabbi from about 1902 to 1970, and was a living model of Judaism for me. I intended to carry on this rabbinic tradition. Another source of my Jewish passion has been my parents, as noted in the dedication of this book. And the third personal source has been Dennis Prager, with whom I have had a unique friendship—both intellectually and emotionally. We have struggled together over life and Judaism for seventeen years.

Like any passion, my Judaism has its low as well as its high moments. As odd as it may sound to a secular world, some of my life's most gratifying moments have come when

I worked out a satisfactory explanation to a seeming paradox in some Jewish source. On the other hand, there are tough times as well. I am not always at peace with God. Any religious Jew who immerses himself in the tragic aspects of Jewish history and the suffering human condition in general, feels included in Elie Wiesel's observation that "the Jew may love God, or he may fight with God; but he may not ignore God."

Yet that is exactly what most contemporary Jews have been doing—ignoring God and Judaism. It is enough that one generation ignore Judaism for the next generation to have terrible misconceptions about it and its goals. For thousands of years, Jews have daily recited their mission, "to perfect the world under the rule of God." The purpose of Jewish existence is not to eat Jewish foods, or tell Jewish jokes, or use Yiddish words. It is to fight evil and to reduce suffering in the world. It is a source of deep pain to me to recognize how few people know this.

This book is meant to set the record straight. For non-Jews as well as Jews. For the airline stewardess. And for her Jewish ex-boyfriend as well.

—JOSEPH TELUSHKIN

Question 1

CAN ONE DOUBT GOD'S EXISTENCE AND STILL BE A GOOD JEW?

> *God may have His own reasons for denying us certainty with regard to His existence and nature. One reason apparent to us is that man's certainty with regard to anything is poison to his soul. Who knows this better than moderns who have had to cope with dogmatic Fascists, Communists, and even scientists?*
>
> —EMANUEL RACKMAN, in *The Condition of Jewish Belief*

> *If the believer has his troubles with evil, the atheist has more and graver difficulties to contend with. Reality stumps him altogether, leaving him baffled not by one consideration but by many, from the existence of natural law through the instinctual cunning of the insect to the brain of the genius and heart of the prophet. This then is the intellectual reason for believing in God: That, though this belief is not free from difficulties, it stands out, head and shoulders, as the best answer to the riddle of the universe.*
>
> —MILTON STEINBERG, *Anatomy of Faith*

17

DOUBT

Does God exist? This is life's most crucial question. The implications of the conclusion have the most significant consequences for the meaning of human existence.

Yet, despite its overwhelming importance, serious discussion of God is usually confined to theologians and philosophers. The rest of us form simple opinions of belief, agnosticism, or atheism at a relatively early age and are content to retain them without questioning for the rest of our lives.

We must therefore begin our presentation of Judaism with a discussion about God. First, let us briefly note Judaism's attitude toward a most common contemporary sentiment about God: doubt.

Can you doubt God's existence and still be a good Jew? Yes.

Belief in God is often difficult. Crises of faith are to be expected, and acknowledging such crises is not an irreligious act for a Jew. There are four significant reasons why doubts about God's existence should not be an obstacle to your being a good Jew.

1. JUDAISM EMPHASIZES DEED OVER CREED

Judaism stresses action far more than faith. The Talmud attributes to God a declaration which is probably unique among religious writings: "Better that they [the Jews] abandon Me, but follow My laws" (for, the Talmud adds, by practicing Judaism's laws, the Jews will return to God, *Jerusalem Talmud Haggigah* 1:7). According to Judaism, one can be a good Jew while doubting God's existence, so long as one acts in accordance with Jewish law. But the converse does not hold true, for a Jew who believes in God but acts contrary to Jewish law cannot be considered a good Jew.

It is not, of course, our intention to deny the centrality of God in Judaism, but merely to emphasize that Judaism can be appreciated and practiced independently of one's present level of belief in God. You can incorporate Judaism into your daily life through study and practice even while doubting God's existence, because Jewish study and practice in and of themselves are extraordinarily valuable to the individual and society.

Moreover, our experience has confirmed that once you begin to study and live Judaism, you will find belief in God much more feasible. As the Talmud notes, whereas a man or woman may begin to practice Judaism for reasons unrelated to God (such as rational and ethical conviction), he or she will eventually do so because of God (*Pesahim* 50b).

2. Absolute certainty in faith leads to fanaticism

In the words of Emanuel Rackman, one of the foremost Orthodox rabbis of our time: "Judaism encourages doubt even as it enjoins faith and commitment. A Jew dare not live with absolute certainty, because certainty is the hallmark of the fanatic and Judaism abhors fanaticism, [and] because doubt is good for the human soul, its humility. . . . God may have had His own reasons for denying us certainty with regard to His existence and nature. One apparent reason is that man's certainty with regard to anything is poison to his soul. Who knows this better than moderns who have had to cope with dogmatic Fascists, Communists, and even scientists?"*

---

* In Milton Himmelfarb, ed., *The Condition of Jewish Belief* (New York: Macmillan, 1966), p. 179.

3. If God were known, moral choice would end

If we *knew* God existed and would punish us for evil acts, then good acts would be much less freely chosen. An element of unknowability about God is necessary so as to allow us to *choose* good. In order to choose good, we must feel free to do bad, and we would not feel this way if we had definite knowledge that God was present and recording our every action. (How much choice do we have to speed when we know a police car is present?)

4. Since God's existence is unprovable, doubt is natural

God cannot be known to exist in the sense that we know a table or a cat exists. Their existences can be physically demonstrated and verified through our senses. But God's existence cannot, since God possesses no physical qualities. *One can prove the existence of the natural, the physical, the finite; God, however, is supernatural, metaphysical, infinite.* The inability to prove God's existence reflects, then, only on the fact that God has no physical qualities, a position that Judaism has always maintained.*

To have doubts about God is, then, normal, permissible, and consistent with being a good Jew. But a good Jew may not *deny God's existence.* Indeed, the primary task of the Jewish people since its inception has been to bring the idea of a universal God and morality, or ethical monotheism, to mankind. As we shall see below, the most important values of life are dependent upon positing the existence of God: morality, or good and evil as objective realities that transcend personal and national opinions, and ultimate purpose and meaning to human existence. To put it another way, if there

---

* The third of Maimonides's Thirteen Principles of the Jewish Faith is that God has no physical qualities. Cf. *Deuteronomy* 4:12.

is no God, then there can be no objective good and evil, and no ultimate purpose to our existence. For these reasons, among many others, a committed Jew (a) may not deny God's existence, (b) must struggle with his doubts about God (the name of the Jewish people, Israel, means "struggle with God"), and (c) must advocate ethical monotheism, the ideal of a universal God as the basis of a universal standard of ethical behavior. As Elie Wiesel stated it: "The Jew may love God, or he may fight with God, but he may not ignore God."

THE NEED TO POSIT GOD'S EXISTENCE

MORALITY

The first value whose existence is dependent upon positing God's existence is morality. If there is no God, there are no rights and wrongs that transcend personal preference. Gases and molecules, the laws of nature, are not "good" or "evil," "right" or "wrong." If the natural world is the one objective reality, and there is no moral source beyond nature, good and evil possess no objective reality. Moral judgments then become purely subjective. They are popular or personal opinions which are objectively meaningless and represent no reality. It is self-evident and acknowledged by the foremost atheist philosophers that if a moral God does not exist, neither does a universal morality. Without God, all we can have are *opinions* about morality, but our opinions about "good" and "evil" behavior are no more valid or binding than our opinions about "good" and "bad" ice cream.

This is why in secular societies morality is generally considered to be a matter of opinion. Moral relativism is the only possible consequence of the denial of God's existence; morality becomes a euphemism for personal opinion. As this century's most eloquent atheist philosopher, Bertrand Russell, wrote: "I cannot see how to refute the arguments for the subjectivity of ethical values but," Russell conceded, "I find myself incapable of believing that all that is wrong with wanton cruelty is that I don't like it."*

Russell's second point is our whole point. All that can possibly be wrong with wanton cruelty according to atheism and its moral relativism, is that we may personally not like it. *Amorality is inherent to atheism.*†

To illustrate this point, assume there is no God and attempt to explain why Hitler was morally wrong. For the atheist and moral relativist, the only thing wrong with Nazi atrocities, as Russell said, "is that I don't like it."

One may answer that we know "deep down" that Hitler's mass murder and torture were wrong. But from where does this "deep down" feeling of right and wrong come? If there is no God, such feelings are just feelings, and objective morality must transcend subjective feelings. And if in fact we do possess "deep down" knowledge of good and evil, what source of morality put it within us?

Or, one may answer that Nazi-type murder is wrong for pragmatic reasons—citing the argument that "if we kill them, they'll start to kill us and society will fall apart." This is not a moral argument, but merely a pragmatic one, and it is in any event invalid, since committing evil can be regarded as

---

* Cited in Germaine Brée, *Camus and Sartre* (New York. Dell Publishing Co., 1972), p. 15.

† Amorality means, of course, no morality, not immorality. Thus, we recognize that good atheists can and do exist. But do their moral values emanate from a secular-based morality, or from three thousand years of religion-based morality? (See pp. 73–74.)

highly practical. In fact, pragmatic arguments usually favor committing the crime. The Nazis, for example, would have correctly dismissed the argument that "if we kill them, then they will kill us" by noting that "they" will not be able to kill "us." As in the rest of nature, only the weak will be destroyed. The pragmatic argument against committing evil is naive. If you can get away with a crime, there is no pragmatic argument against committing it—only a moral argument, which is often quite impractical.

Take, for example, the relatively minor crime of tax evasion. The pragmatic argument again argues *for*, not against, committing the crime. The argument that "if everyone cheated on their tax returns, we would all suffer," understandably dissuades almost no one from cheating. On the contrary, tax evaders are quite certain that nearly everyone else *is* cheating, and it is precisely this fact that serves as their justification for doing the same. Precisely because one believes nearly everyone else is cheating, he, too, should cheat. Otherwise he loses. Pragmatism dictates immoral behavior at least as often as it dictates moral behavior.

Or, one may answer that *reason* tells us that Hitler was wrong, and, that in general, evil is wrong. Reason, according to this common attitude, suffices to lead us to moral behavior without the necessity of positing the existence of God. But is this so?

REASON OFTEN SUGGESTS EVIL BEHAVIOR

Reason rarely argues for moral behavior. In fact, reason can nearly always be used to justify immoral behavior—from supporting Nazism to petty cheating in everyday life. The use of reason to justify what is wrong is so common that we have a special word for it—*rationalization*.

Adolph Eichmann and other Nazi murderers acted "reasonably" when they obeyed orders to murder people and thereby furthered their careers. When the average German citizen remained silent while his Jewish neighbors were shipped to concentration camps, he was acting entirely according to reason. Reason suggested preserving one's life and not endangering it by aiding a Jew. It may in fact be argued that among the only people in Nazi Germany who acted against reason were those who acted morally.

To cite a more mundane example, according to the *New York Times,* one out of every three hotel guests steals something from his room. Since it is probable that most of these people consider stealing immoral, are we to assume that millions of Americans consider themselves thieves? No. Undoubtedly most will deny that what they have done is thievery; they *rationalize* their actions by claiming that the hotel overcharges, or that "everyone else" also takes "souvenirs," or that the towel (or ashtray, or painting) will not be missed.

In sum, *reason is amoral.* It is a human tool that can be used as easily for evil as for good.

REASON CANNOT DEMAND GOOD BEHAVIOR (EVEN WHEN IT SUGGESTS IT)

The preceding examples should make it obvious that if reason often does not even suggest good behavior, it cannot possibly be relied upon to demand good behavior. And even when reason does argue for moral behavior, it is not reason that compels a person to act morally. Reason may very well have *suggested* to many Germans during World War II that they actively oppose Nazism and to many Americans that they not steal from their hotel rooms, but it in no way would *compel* them to act accordingly. And for the few Germans who did actively oppose Nazism, it was not reason that dictated their moral behavior. It was a recognition of something higher than reason that compelled them to act morally.

Thus, given these two facts, that reason can suggest evil, and that it cannot compel good behavior even when it suggests it, we can accurately characterize the notion that reason alone can or will produce moral behavior as a dangerous myth.

To return to our original question: If there is no God whose moral will transcends personal opinion, then we cannot say that Hitler was morally wrong. All we can say is "I don't like it."*

The source of morality must itself be moral, and since reason is amoral, it cannot be the source of morality. That source must be something higher than reason. From the time the Jews stood at Mount Sinai to this day, that higher source has been called God.

ULTIMATE PURPOSE

Morality is not the only value whose existence is dependent upon positing the existence of God. If the physical world is the only reality, i.e., if there is no metaphysical source to life, then life is ultimately purposeless. Life is then nothing more than the chance result of innumerable coincidences, and human beings are nothing more than self-aware molecules. We differ from all other molecular combinations only in that we want to believe that our particular combination has

---

* None of the foregoing should be interpreted as an abandonment of reason in either the moral or religious spheres. It is reason *alone*, reason without a higher source of morality, without ethical monotheism, that allows or leads to evil. Likewise, faith in God by itself allows or leads to evil. Reason without religion gave us Communism, and religion without reason gave us the Crusades and Qaddafi.

some ultimate meaning and purpose. But this desire is mere delusion. We simply cannot bear to awaken each morning and look in the mirror at a molecular coincidence, so we make up a meaning to our lives.

The purposelessness of life if there is no God is not some argument created by theologians. It is a fact, and it underlies all secular existentialist thought. The argument of secular existentialism develops as follows: Given that God does not exist, life is mere physical coincidence with no meaning. Hence, we must endow our "being and nothingness," to use the well-chosen words of Jean-Paul Sartre, with some arbitrary meaning, or we cannot survive the pain of life.

For the Jew, the physical world is very real. But it is not the only reality. There is a metaphysical reality as well. The source of this metaphysical reality, God, has created the physical reality and has endowed the human being with a touch of the divine. This element can be called spirituality, or soul, or the image of God, or sanctity. By any name, it means the same: We are not purposeless physical creations of a cruel and apathetic universe, but purposeful spiritual creations of a loving and just God.

In order, then, to spread a universal standard of good and evil in the world, and because the death of belief in God must lead to moral chaos and a pervasive sense of meaninglessness, the Jew must posit and advance ethical monotheism even when he is in doubt about God. God's existence is demonstrably necessary for a moral world and for ultimate meaning to life.

Nevertheless, one may conclude that while God's existence is clearly *necessary*, belief in God's existence is irrational and even perhaps impossible. Let us therefore address ourselves to the question of the *probability* of God's existence.

DOES GOD EXIST?

There are strong arguments on both sides of this question, but in our view the case for the existence of God is stronger than the atheist argument.

To paraphrase an argument of Milton Steinberg, *the believer in God must account for one thing, the existence of evil; the atheist, however, must account for the existence of everything else.*

The problem of evil is the most difficult and troubling challenge to religious faith, and any advocate of a religious world view must constantly agonize over it. Before responding to this, however, let us counter with Steinberg's challenge to the nonbeliever: If there is no God, how do you account for the existence of all the *good* in the world? For consciousness and conscience? Intelligence? Emotions? Love? The laws of nature? For our sense of purpose to the world? For all creation? For the very notion of a universal good and evil?

Those of us who affirm God's existence regard such nonphysical realities as emanating from a higher nonphysical source, God. How does the atheist account for all these phenomena? Generally, the atheist will explain that they have developed through coincidences such as the random couplings of gases and molecules. In fact, *everything*, according to the atheist, developed by chance.*

---

* Even if the atheist claims that he has no specific way to explain the origins of these phenomena, but that one day science will provide these answers, the atheist still ascribes everything to chance, since he holds that impersonal random forces constitute the ultimate cause of good, pleasure, consciousness, intelligence, and so on. Science will undoubtedly supply us with more information, but science describes only *processes*, and processes have no relevance to the questions of who or what is behind these techniques, or *for what purpose* these techniques and life in general exist.

Now we do admit that beauty, love, art, intelligence, consciousness, conscience, natural laws, complex cellular activity, the pervasive sense of purpose, the notions of universal justice and morality, and all creation could emanate from inanimate coincidences. But while this is a possibility, logic and reason (not to mention our religious natures) compel us to reject it as a probability. Design suggests to us a Designer, law a Lawgiver, creation a Creator, intelligence a Source of intelligence, conscience a God.

There are two possible explanations for creation: that everything comes from chance and coincidence, or from design and purpose. The choice is between nonsense and sense. If there is no God, one cannot speak of sense in life, or of good and evil, or of ultimate purpose. These things would be, as we have noted, mere delusions created by our minds to deny that all is anarchic and meaningless.

But the moment you affirm that these nonphysical aspects of life possess an objective reality, you are implicitly affirming the existence of God. From where else do these nonphysical realities derive? Gases and amino acids do not possess truth, purpose, good, or evil.

As Milton Steinberg wrote: "This then is the intellectual reason for believing in God: that though this belief is not free from difficulties, it stands out, head and shoulders, as the best answer to the riddle of the universe."*

There is, however, one other riddle that is best explained by positing the existence of God; the existence and impact of the Jews. The history, survival, and most mysterious of all, the overwhelming impact upon history of the Jews cannot be explained by the criteria applied to any other nation's fate.

---

* *Anatomy of Faith* (New York: Harcourt Brace, 1960), pp. 88–96.

First, there are the unparalleled facts of Jewish survival as a distinct people. In all the world, only the Jews have survived for nearly four thousand years with their culture intact. Only the Jews have had their homeland destroyed (twice), been dispersed throughout the world and homeless for two thousand years, endured hatred wherever they have lived, survived the most systematic attempt in history (aside from that on the Gypsies) to destroy an entire people, and been expelled from nearly every nation among whom they have lived. Yet the Jews still live, studying about their ancestors who lived about 1600 B.C.E., having the same homeland as in 1000 B.C.E., speaking there the same language as their ancestors did over three thousand years ago, and worshiping the same God.

The enigma of Jewish survival has perplexed nearly all world historians and social philosophers. Among the latter, perhaps Mark Twain expressed it most succinctly: "The Egyptian, the Babylonian, and the Persian rose, filled the planet with sound and splendor, then faded to dreamstuff and passed away; the Greek and the Roman followed and made a vast noise, and they are gone; other peoples have sprung up and held their torch high for a time, but it burned out, and they sit in twilight now or have vanished. The Jew saw them all, beat them all, and is now what he always was, exhibiting no decadence, no infirmities of age, no weakening of his parts, no slowing of his energies, no dulling of his alert and aggressive mind. All things are mortal but the Jew: all other forces pass, but he remains. What is the secret of his immortality?"*

---

* *Harper's Magazine*, September 1899.

For the Jew, of course, "the secret of his immortality" is the divine element in Jewish history.

But there is something far more perplexing and impressive than the survival of the Jews, and that is the influence which this people has had upon humanity. A tiny group of uncultured and homeless slaves gave the world God, ethical monotheism, the concept of universal moral responsibility, the notion of human sanctity (human creation in "the image of God"), the idea of progress (linear as opposed to cyclical history),* messianism, the Prophets, the Bible, and the Ten Commandments. If not for the Jews, there would be no Christianity, no Islam, no Marxism, no socialism, no humanism. It is no wonder that Jew-haters have so constantly spoken of a world Jewish conspiracy.

The greatest powers in the world have always seemed to be obsessed with this numerically insignificant people. The Romans, the Church, the Nazis, the Communist world, the Muslim world, and the United Nations have each, for long periods of time, been preoccupied with the Jews. To this day, this people, which numbers less than 14 million in a world of over 4.5 billion people, or fewer than three out of every thousand people, is at the center of human events.

To the Jew himself, the reason for the Jewish impact upon mankind has always been clear. The Jew is inherently no different from any other human being, and any other human being can become a Jew. Hence, the explanation for the Jewish impact is not to be found in the Jews themselves but

---

* "Judaism repudiated the cyclic view of history held by all other ancient peoples and affirmed that it was a meaningful process leading to the gradual regeneration of humanity. This was the origin of the Western belief in progress. . . ." (Henry Bamford Parkes, *The Divine Order: Western Culture in the Middle Ages and the Renaissance*, New York: Alfred A. Knopf, 1969, p. 14.)

in Judaism. Something else must be at play in Jewish history and in the Jewish impact upon world history: something beyond history—perhaps God. When one begins to appreciate fully the uniqueness of the monotheist ideal, its seemingly spontaneous generation in the minds of human beings at only one time among only one people, and the utterly unique impact of Judaism upon the world, one concludes that either superhuman beings or God was the initiator of Judaism and ethical monotheism. God seems more plausible.

ATHEISM

To set forth certain arguments for the existence of God is not in itself sufficient, because it does not take into account the nature of many atheists and some of their reasons for atheism. Atheists may be classified under one or more of five categories.

1. ATHEISTS WHO DENY GOD BECAUSE GOD WAS PRESENTED TO THEM IN A CHILDISH OR DISTORTED MANNER

It is unfortunate but undeniable that God is often perceived and presented in a foolish or distorted manner. A typical example is the anthropomorphic conception of God which portrays Him as, for example, a grand old man sitting up in heaven. Such a straw-man God is a convenient target for atheists' jibes at believers; it was this caricature that Soviet cosmonauts mocked when they boasted that up in space they saw no God.

A second common distortion is the portrayal of God as little more than a cosmic butler, someone to call on to grant our requests, someone whose reason for being is to serve us rather than we Him.

The third and worst distortion of God takes place when evil is committed in His name. This is a favorite theme of atheists who cite Church atrocities as examples of the moral irrelevance of God.* This argument, however, poses little problem to Judaism, since it does not claim that faith in God by itself produces good people or a good world. God is the basis of morality, but in order to become a moral person and make a more moral world, two other commitments *must* accompany a commitment to God: commitments to the supremacy of morality and the use of reason.

Moreover, if we are to negate God because certain individuals or groups have committed evil in God's name, then we must likewise negate laws, science, sex, and any other noble goal or fact of life. Laws can put criminals in prison, but they can also, as in Nazi Germany and the Soviet Union, put criminals in power. Science can cure millions, but it can also destroy millions. Sex can be beautiful, but there are rapists. The fact that men can pervert the name of God, or corrupt laws, science, and sex, only bears witness to the human potential to corrupt. Because we can pervert God, morality, and reason, does not mean we can do without them.

Therefore, we invite atheists who identify themselves in this category to examine the conception of God held in Jewish sources. Judaism brought the one-God concept into the world. Atheists will discover that the anthropomorphic or cosmic butler conceptions of God are utterly foreign to

---

* Considering the fact that it was the Jews who suffered the greatest atrocities at the hands of the Church, one would think that this argument should appeal more to Jews than to anyone else. Obviously it has not; the fact that their torturers spoke of God made no impact on the martyred Jews' beliefs whatsoever. It only served to reconfirm the urgency of the Jewish role in the world.

Judaism. When Moses confronted God, he asked Him His name. "I am what I am," God replied. The Jew cannot know *what* God is, only *that* God is and what God wants.

2. ATHEISTS WHO DENY GOD IN REBELLION AGAINST THEIR HOME, BACKGROUND, PARENTS, OR EXTERNAL AUTHORITY IN GENERAL

The rejection of a parent's religion or God is a common feature of the assertion of independence from parental influence. This rejection of God is not limited to the children of authoritarian homes; it is equally prevalent in children from overly permissive homes. The children of very lenient parents are also likely to revolt against external authority. The children to whom parents gave "everything" came to see *themselves* as the ultimate being, thus rejecting all need for any higher authority—be it a parent, a school, a government, or God.

3. ATHEISTS WHO DENY GOD BECAUSE THEY WERE RAISED IN AND/OR LIVE IN A SECULAR ENVIRONMENT

Though few atheists may admit it, many of them learned their views concerning God and religion in their homes as they grew up, and they have rarely, if ever, questioned them. Atheists rightly dismiss the beliefs of many religious individuals as little more than ingrained attitudes derived from the home or social environment. But atheists who have not sought to confront intelligent believers and their arguments, and who have not tested their denials of God in living situations among sophisticated religious people, are subject to the same dismissal.

Therefore, the atheist who seeks truth, a better self, and a better world is obligated to seek out religious people and religious literature before locking himself into atheist dogma.

Intellectual honesty and moral concern demand this approach.

4. ATHEISTS WHO DENY GOD BECAUSE OF PERSONAL SUFFERING OR HUMAN SUFFERING IN GENERAL

There is not much we can say to someone who denies the existence of God because of personal tragedy such as the death or suffering of loved ones. To these people we must offer an extended hand, not arguments.

Nevertheless, the denial of God's existence after personal tragedy constitutes more of an emotional than a rational response to the question of God. Our periods of suffering do not disprove God's existence any more than our moments of joy prove it.

Moreover, we must be specific when speaking of human suffering. We must distinguish between two causes, human and natural, for only the second directly questions God's existence.

Man-made evil. Let us take a most terrible problem for Jews today, faith after Auschwitz. How can be believe in God after He allowed six million Jews, including over a million children, to be gassed, burned, experimented on, frozen, and transformed into soap bars and lampshades? There is virtually no Jew who has not asked this question.

Before offering some thoughts on this question, a personal note is in order. Though we (the authors) were both born in the United States after the Holocaust, and though neither of us lost any immediate family in the Holocaust, the Holocaust has had the most profound impact on our thinking. Part of each one of us died with the six million. Nevertheless, the Holocaust does not constitute an insurmountable obstacle to our belief in God. First, and foremost,

God did not build Auschwitz and its crematoria. Men did. Man, not God, is responsible for the Holocaust. Judaism posits that people have freedom of choice. Perhaps we would prefer that people had been created as robots who could do only good rather than as human beings who can also choose evil. But this is impossible; only where there exists the possibility of evil does there exist the possibility of good.

Secondly, while the Holocaust may suggest to us Jews denial of God, to what do we attribute the survival of the Jewish people, its massive impact on the world, and the rise of Israel?

Thirdly, *the Holocaust may make faith in God difficult; but it makes faith in man impossible.* Along with the six million Jews, and tens of millions of others murdered by the Nazis and Communists, we must bury the doctrine which enabled Communism and Nazism to rise: the belief that man is the highest being. After Auschwitz and the Gulag Archipelago, we have two choices: belief in man under God or belief in nothing.

The question to be posed after Auschwitz, Gulag Archipelago, and other such barbarities is not "Where was God?" but "Where is man?"

Natural suffering. With natural suffering (disease, earthquakes, etc.) we face a far more difficult problem than with man-made suffering. True, man does have the capacity to greatly limit natural suffering, and in some cases, even to eliminate it, and man must therefore share part of the responsibility for the prevalence of natural suffering.

Nevertheless, we readily admit that the issue of natural suffering is the most difficult one confronting the believer in God. We do not know why God allows (or perhaps even creates) natural suffering.

This does not mean, however, that Judaism is silent on the issue of natural suffering. On the contrary, an entire book of the Bible, *Job*, is devoted to the subject. *Job* recounts the terrible sufferings endured by a man whom the Bible emphasizes was a particularly good and righteous man (thereby making the question of his suffering even sharper), and it details the questions and explanations offered by Job and his friends concerning human suffering and God. The Book of *Job* asks: If God is good, why do good people suffer?

Job's friends are of the opinion that the suffering of Job (as a symbol of all people) is punishment for his sins. But the Bible, i.e., Judaism, categorically rejects this notion.

Why, then, do good people suffer? After thirty-seven tense chapters of questioning and challenging, of bitterness and tears, God gives Job, and us, His answer:

> *Then God answered Job . . . and said:*
> *"Who is this that complicates ideas*
> *With words without knowledge?*
> *Get prepared like a man,*
> *I will ask you and you tell me.*
> *Where were you when I established the world?*
> *Tell me, if you know so much.*
> *Who drafted its dimensions? Do you know? . . .*
> *Did you ever command forth a morning? . . .*
> *Have death's gates been revealed to you?*
> *Have you examined earth's expanse?*
> *Tell me, if you know.*
> *Can you . . . guide the bear with her cubs? . . .*
> *Does the hawk soar by your wisdom?*
> *Does the eagle mount at your command,*
> *And make his nest on high? . . ."*
> *God answered Job and said:*
> *"Will the contender with God yield?*
> *He who reproves God, let him answer for it."*

Job answered God and said:
"Lo, I am small, how can I answer you?
My hand I lay on my mouth.
I have spoken once, I will not reply . . .
I talked of things I did not know,
Wonders beyond my ken. . . ."
                    (*Job* 38:1-4, 12, 17-18, 32; 40:1-5)

God's answer? God is God, and who are we to assume that we can understand everything? As an ancient Hebrew phrase put it: "If I knew Him [God], I'd be Him." Who "established the world," we or God? Admittedly, this may not be the answer we hoped for, but *what answer would we desire?* If God is God and man is man, is there any other possible answer than the one given to Job?

Certainly, Judaism could have presented a more "popular" image of God, or denied the reality of suffering (as was done often in Eastern philosophies), or theologically explained human suffering as divinely ordained punishment, but it does not do this.

To the rational and thinking person, this very honesty of Judaism, its unwillingness to compromise on the nature of God despite its desire to gain adherents, is very reassuring. In Judaism, we can affirm the existence of God without suspending either our reason or our questioning. Indeed, for the Jew, reason and questioning should ultimately be a source of affirmation that there *is* a God, and that ultimately there *is* meaning to my life—and yes, even to my suffering.

5. ATHEISTS WHO DENY GOD BECAUSE THEY HAVE EXPLORED BOTH SIDES OF THE ISSUE

There remains a very small minority of atheists who do not fall into the first four categories. These individuals have come to the conclusion that there is no God neither out of blind acceptance of an atheistic doctrine handed down to them, nor out of rebellion against home and environment, nor because God has been presented to them foolishly, nor out of an emotional reaction to tragedy, but after efforts to believe and lead a religious life, after reading intelligent presentations of the concept of God, and after sustained dialogue with sophisticated believers.

Frankly, we have never met such people, though through their writings we are aware of the existence of such individuals. Yet even these few extraordinary atheists still ascribe the existence of everything to chance; and most important, they still confront the greatest challenge to atheism: It renders morality subjective. As Dostoevsky wrote in *The Brothers Karamazov*, "where there is no God, all is permitted." Atheism denies God, but what does it affirm?

The answer is, of course, that atheism affirms nothing —though this does not mean that atheists affirm nothing. On the contrary, atheists replace God with gods of their own choosing: humanity, art, reason, the state, secular ideologies, science, progress, revolution, culture, education, happiness, the self. . . . The issue is not belief or nonbelief, but belief in God or belief in other gods.

At great cost in human life and suffering, however, we have learned that all these other gods have failed; that *without God each of these substitute values is meaningless and ultimately terribly dangerous* because they become ends in themselves, beyond good and evil.

CONCLUSION

Atheism, then, is rationally no more (and apparently a good deal less) convincing an answer to the mysteries of human existence and the universe than is belief in God. On this issue, Voltaire, himself an unrelenting antagonist of organized religion, said: "In the opinion that there is a God, there are difficulties; but in the contrary opinion there are absurdities."

Atheism not only suffers from a lack of answers and from amorality; it is for most of its adherents an intellectually lazy doctrine as well. Despite the fact that to many people atheism is usually associated with intellect, the majority of atheists have no more questioned their beliefs than most simple believers have questioned theirs.

Many Jews today have doubts about God's existence, but they *live* as if God does not exist. They are agnostics, but live as atheists. But there are compelling intellectual, moral, and existential reasons to live as if God does exist—to live a Jewish life—even when you have doubts.

You may be an agnostic in theory, but in practice you live either a Jewish life or a secular life. Of course the primary concern of this book, as we see in the next chapter, is with living a Jewish life. It is through living a Jewish life, even while struggling with one's doubts, that one becomes a good Jew.

Question 2

Why Do We Need Organized Religion or Jewish Laws—Isn't It Enough to Be a Good Person?

> . . . The purpose of the laws of the Torah
> is to promote compassion, loving-kindness
> and peace in the world.
> —Moses Maimonides (1135–1204),
> Yad Hazakah, Hilkhot Shabbat 2:3

We need organized religion for the same reason we need organized political parties, or any organized social movement. Whether it be to attain national independence, elect a particular candidate, or, in the case of Judaism, perfect the world through ethical monotheism, people with similar values and goals must organize themselves in order to have an effect upon the world.

Why, then, if we recognize the need for organization in so many areas of social concern, does it seem illogical or undesirable to many people that there be organization in religion?

The answer lies in the understanding that most people have of religion, organized or not. They regard religion as an institution that regulates prayer and other rituals, and which demands certain beliefs about God. Consequently, many individuals feel that religion is or should be a "private affair," and that organized religion is unnecessary since private affairs need not be organized.

It may very well be that the religion to which many people have been exposed consists of little more than prayer, ritual, and belief, and in such cases we agree that organized religion is largely organized irrelevance. But this type of religion has little in common with Judaism. Judaism is concerned with organizing people to better the world. It is an all-encompassing value- and action-shaping way of life whose goal is the creation of a moral and holy* nation† which in turn morally

---

* Holiness, kedusha in Hebrew, is a concept which originated with Judaism and which is unique to religion. Secular ideologies cannot possess the concept of holiness because it transcends the material world, the only reality that atheism recognizes as having an objective existence. Kedusha

42

improves the world, and whose means are the laws (*mitzvot*) of Judaism.

In order to realize this goal, all those individuals who are committed to it must organize themselves. Some did, about 3,500 years ago, and they are known as Jews. Thus, Judaism is not at all an "organized religion" in the usual sense. The Jews are an organized group of people from every racial and ethnic background who are committed to the Jewish way of perfecting the world.

ISN'T IT ENOUGH TO BE A GOOD PERSON?

The term "good person" is commonly misused today. Often after advocating the adoption of a religious-ethical system, we are challenged by questioners who claim to "know good people who do not believe in [and thus presumably do not need] religion." When asked to define a good person, these people

basically implies the elevation of the human being and human actions from animal-like to God-like (see pp. 49–52).

† There is some understandable confusion concerning this issue: Are the Jews a nation or a religion? The Jews are, and always have been, both. This is unique in today's world, but in the ancient world, of which the Jews are the one surviving intact culture, it was common for a nation to have a religion that was unique to it. To this day, the Jews remain a nation defined by its religion: even secular Jews recognize that one cannot be a Christian or Muslim Jew, that by becoming a member of the Christian or Muslim *religion*, one is no longer a member of the Jewish *nation*. Similarly, all Jews recognize that a member of any nation can become a member of the Jewish nation only by converting to the Jewish religion. On the other hand, a completely irreligious Jew is as much a Jew as the most religious one, because Jews are also a nation. Thus, an American Jew is a member of two nations, the American and the Jewish—though his only country or state is the United States. Attempts by Jews or non-Jews to tear the national or religious limb from Judaism have resulted in the assimilation or destruction of Jews.

generally answer "someone who doesn't hurt anybody." We are convinced that most people define a good person as one who does not hurt anyone. This definition is as wrong, however, as it is popular. *A person whose conduct consists of not hurting anyone is not good; such a person is merely not bad.* To be a good person involves the *active* pursuit of good. It is not enough merely to refrain from hurting other human beings; one must intercede on their behalf: "Do not stand by while your neighbor's blood is shed" (*Leviticus* 19:16). Nor is it enough to refrain from personally performing an injustice, for in order to be good one must seek out and rectify injustices performed by others: "Justice, justice you shall pursue" (*Deuteronomy* 16:20); "And you shall burn the evil from out of your midst" (*Deuteronomy* 17:7 and elsewhere).

The insufficiency of defining goodness as not hurting others is clearly demonstrated by the general assessment of the behavior of most Germans under the Nazis. According to this definition, most Germans during the Holocaust were good people, since they did not hurt anyone. Yet most of us do not consider such Germans good people, clearly indicating that we recognize the impossibility of defining a good person as one who does not hurt anyone.

You do not have to do something bad in order to do bad; you have only to do nothing.

This is why Judaism consists of so many *positive* laws of goodness. The Jew is commanded to give charity, silence gossip, visit the sick. In contrast, secular laws are almost all *negative* laws, not to commit criminal acts. There are very few secular laws demanding good acts (nor do we wish to see many such laws passed; hence the ideal of religious individuals and a nonreligious government).

Judaism has developed what has come to be the most

extensive system of legislated good known to mankind (see, for example, the laws of charity in the appendix). When one considers all these moral imperatives, it becomes clear that most people are good only by the passive definition of "not hurting anybody," while their goodness is deficient by Judaism's definition of active involvement—be it helping Cambodian and Vietnamese boat people, retarded children, or Soviet Jews and other Soviet dissidents, opposing totalitarianism, or actively assisting any good cause unrelated to their immediate lives. Most of us are quite content to lead lives uncommitted to much other than ourselves.

For this reason, the great majority of people need a system of laws of ethics. Even the minority of people which is preoccupied with moral issues could use such a system. As Judaism long ago realized, and as twentieth-century man must realize now, *moral ideals do not suffice to create moral individuals and a moral world.* Judaism's ideals of universal peace and justice are by now virtually universally accepted ideals, and numerous ideologies (e.g., Christianity, Marxism, socialism, humanism) have arisen promising to realize these ideals, but without a legal-ethical system such as Judaism's binding on their adherents. However, all the horrors perpetrated in the name of ideals constitute tragic but irrefutable testimony that ideals are not enough and that a detailed system of ethical laws binding upon every individual is indispensable to achieving peace, justice, and brotherhood.

To be better at anything—from a sport to an art—a system is necessary. Why not a system for goodness?

There are of course any number of people who do not observe Jewish law and who are actively good. Although we commend the adoption of Judaism and its laws to them as well for even greater ethical proficiency, Judaism holds that for the non-Jew this goodness is quite "enough,"* and that such a non-Jew has a "portion of the world to come" (*Tosefta Sanhedrin* 13:2) and is entitled to material support from the Jewish community whenever necessary (*Leviticus* 25:35–6). Non-Jews are not obligated to assume the burden of Judaism and its laws (though we are delighted when any do).

Jews, however, are obligated to observe Jewish laws because they are obligated to become as good as is humanly possible, to also become holy, and to keep the Jewish people and its mission alive. To achieve these ends is the task of the Jewish laws, an understanding of which we now offer.

JEWISH LAW

There are four categories of Jewish law. Every Jewish law falls into one or more of these categories.†

---

* In fact, such active goodness is more than "enough," since Judaism holds non-Jews responsible for obeying only what are known as "the seven laws of the children of Noah" (i.e., the laws of mankind, as we are all descended from Noah). Since ancient times these laws have been understood as prohibitions against idolatry, blasphemy, murder, sexual sins (such as incest and adultery), theft, eating a limb torn from a living animal, and the positive commandment to set up a legal system to ensure obedience to the other six laws (see *Sanhedrin* 56A).

† The idea of offering rational explanations for the Jewish laws is foreign to many Jews. There is an unfortunate tendency among both observant and nonobservant Jews to regard many Jewish laws as "rituals" that have no intrinsic rational or ethical meaning. On the one hand, many very observant Jews advocate blind observance of Jewish laws and object to attempts to explain them, fearing that such explanations will make the laws seem human rather than divine in origin. On the other hand, many nonobservant Jews defend their nonobservance by dismissing many Jewish laws as "rituals" devoid of rational and/or ethical purpose. Though they proceed from opposite viewpoints, both types of Jews succeed in keeping the majority of

CATEGORY	PURPOSE
Reflexive Laws	To elevate the performer of the law
Laws of Ethics	To ensure moral treatment of others
Laws of Holiness	To elevate human actions from animal-like to God-like
National Laws	To identify with the Jewish nation and with its past

REFLEXIVE LAWS

Every act we perform affects us. We often lose sight of this, but the fact is that our actions influence us at least as much as we influence our actions.

Every Jewish law affects the performer, but there are certain Jewish laws whose purpose is almost exclusively to

---

Jews ignorant of, and estranged from, that aspect of Judaism which most renders it unique—Jewish law. This is a tragedy, for when Jews are taught the reasons for Jewish laws, they begin to observe them. This unwillingness to seek out the meaning and purpose of Jewish law was denounced eight hundred years ago by Moses Maimonides, in his masterwork, the *Guide to the Perplexed* (Part 3, Chapter 31): "There is a group of human beings who consider it a grievous thing that causes should be given for any law; what would please them most is that the intellect would not find a meaning for the commandments and prohibitions. What compels them to feel thus is a sickness that they find in their souls, a sickness to which they are unable to give utterance and of which they cannot furnish a satisfactory account. For they think that if those laws were useful in this existence and had been given to us for this or that reason, it would be as if they derived from the reflection and understanding of some intelligent being. If, however, there is a thing for which the intellect could not find any meaning at all and that does not lead to something useful, it indubitably derives from God: For the reflection of man would lead to no such thing" (S. Pines' translation of the *Guide*, Chicago: University of Chicago Press, 1963, pp. 523–4). Following in the Maimonidean tradition, the contemporary Anglo-Jewish scholar, Louis Jacobs, has written, ". . . nowhere in the whole of the biblical record is there the faintest suggestion that God imposes upon man arbitrary rules which must be observed purely on the grounds that God so desires" (see Jacobs' essay, "The Relationship Between Religion and Ethics in Jewish Thought" in *Religion and Morality*, edited by Gene Outka and John P. Reeder Jr., New York: 1973, p. 156).

affect the performer. The most obvious example is prayer, whose primary purpose is to affect the person praying. This is why the very word in Hebrew meaning to pray, *l'hitpallel*, is a *reflexive* verb which means "to judge or examine oneself." *God does not need our prayer, we do.* A person who takes time out regularly to examine himself is inevitably affected by the act.

Another example of a reflexive Jewish law is that concerning *tzitzit*, the fringe to be worn at the corners of one's garment. The reflexive purpose of the law is clearly set forth in the Torah: "And God spoke to Moses saying: speak to the children of Israel and tell them to make a *tzitzit* [fringe] on the corners of their garments throughout their generations . . . so that you will see it and remember all the commandments of God and do them . . ." (*Numbers* 15:38–9).

LAWS OF ETHICS
The ultimate purpose of all Jewish law is to produce a good people. To that end, goodness must be both defined and legislated. This Judaism has done. Hundreds of *mitzvot* (commandments) define standards of morality and command the Jew to put them into practice.

Some of these laws of ethics, such as the last six of the Ten Commandments (to honor one's parents, not to murder, commit adultery, steal, bear false witness, or covet), have been adopted by nearly every civilization in the world. However, most of Judaism's other *mitzvot* of ethics have not been adopted. For example, it is a *mitzvah*, or religious duty, to give ten percent of one's annual income to charity. Here is a clear example of the need to define goodness: it would not suffice for Judaism to command the Jew merely to be char-

itable—a specific minimum had to be set, lest we "be chari-
table" with too little.

There is a *mitzvah* in the Talmud that prohibits a Jew
from asking a storekeeper the price of an item which he knows
he will not buy (*Mishnah Bava Metziah* 4:10), thereby raising the hopes of the storekeeper for no reason. While the Jew
is, of course, permitted to comparison-shop, he or she is obligated to consider the feelings of the storekeeper before inquir-
ing about prices. This particular law is not among Judaism's
most important, but when one adds up hundreds of such laws
requiring consideration for our fellow human beings, we
begin to understand why Jews have tended to be obsessed
with moral issues.

There even exists an entire legal text detailing Judaism's
laws governing permitted and nonpermitted speech. Are we
permitted to say anything we want, even when true, about
anyone? Judaism says no. *Lashon ha-rah*, speaking evil about
someone behind his or her back, is a serious sin in Judaism
(see pp. 178–81).

There are also many Jewish laws governing the treatment
of animals. To cite a few examples: the Jew must feed his
animals before himself (*Talmud Berakhot* 40A), give his animals complete rest on the Shabbat, refrain from hunting, and
slaughter those animals which are permitted to be eaten only
in a rigidly specified humane manner.

There are myriad other Jewish laws of ethics, legislating
business relations; treatment of the elderly; care for the weak,
the ill, the poor, and mourners; and conduct in every other
area of life. We are not even permitted to be joyful over the
fall of our enemies: young children at the Passover Seder are
taught to emulate the adults and remove ten drops of wine

from their cups out of sympathy for the ancient Egyptians who suffered under the ten plagues.

It is as difficult to become a good person as it is to become a good artist. That is why observance of the Jewish laws of ethics has not been an easy commitment. But the result is a nation preoccupied with perfecting the world.

LAWS OF HOLINESS

Judaism demands that the Jews be a holy, as well as a moral, people: "And you shall be holy, for I the Lord, your God, am holy" (*Leviticus* 19:2). The purpose of the laws of holiness is to make our actions, and even our time, holy.

The human being is created in God's image, but he is also an animal. Acting like an animal is therefore natural while acting God-like (holy) must be cultivated. This is why there are so many *mitzvot* governing those human activities that are most animal-like. Instead of denying or denigrating our animal-like activities, Judaism attempts to sanctify them through its laws of holiness.

The activities we most obviously share with the animals, and which accordingly have a large number of *mitzvot*, are eating and sexual relations. We can eat or engage in sexual relations just as animals do, or we can elevate the way we engage in those activities. Even in nonreligious life we recognize both our ability to, and the undesirability of, acting like an animal. Thus we say, for example, that someone "eats like a pig," or compare a person who has many sexual partners to a rabbit.

To elevate the act of eating, the most frequent of our animal-like activities, Judaism prescribes numerous *mitzvot*. The Jew must first wash his hands (ceremonially, as well as hygienically), recite a blessing over the washing ("Blessed are

You, God . . . who has *made us holy* with His *mitzvot*, and commanded us about washing our hands [before eating]"), and then recite a blessing of gratitude for the food. He or she is also instructed to speak of Torah-related (moral or holy) matters during the meal, and to recite a blessing of gratitude at the conclusion of the meal. Moreover, the Jew, unlike the animal, is not permitted to eat whatever he wants: The laws of Kashrut limit the Jew's diet to a very few animals.* (Kashrut is more fully explained later on pages 57–64.)

Regarding sexual activities, Judaism likewise attempts to make holy what is naturally animal-like. The Ten Commandments outlaw adultery. Even within marriage, Jewish law does not permit the Jew to engage in sexual relations any time the desire arises. Two thousand years ago, the Talmud forbade the Jewish male to have sexual intercourse with his wife unless she also wished to have relations, and both partners are obligated to abstain from sexual relations for a given period of time each month. If these conditions are met, however, Judaism does not regard the sex act as animal-like; it sees it, rather, as the quintessence of holiness. In fact, the rabbis specifically enjoin couples to make love on the Shabbat. The medieval *Iggeret ha-Kodesh*, attributed to the great thirteenth-century biblical scholar Nachmanides, summarized the Jewish attitude in these words: "When a man is in union with his wife in a spirit of holiness or purity, the Divine presence is with them."

The Jewish laws of holiness not only sanctify actions, they sanctify time as well, prescribing the observance of

---

* These restrictions on the Jew's diet should not be viewed, however, as motivated by asceticism. Jewish law sees sensual and other forms of physical enjoyment as joys, and gifts of God. According to the Talmud, "In the future, a man will be required to give an accounting for every pleasurable food which he could have legitimately experienced, but which he refused to partake of" (*Jerusalem Talmud*, end of *Tractate Kiddushin*).

Shabbat (which is discussed on pages 53–57), and the Jewish holy days and festivals.

To illustrate the concept of sanctifying time and also the difference between a religious and secular lifestyle, let us compare, for example, the Jewish observance of the Jewish New Year (Rosh Ha-Shanah) with the secular celebration of January 1. Whereas the Jewish New Year is two holy days which inaugurate ten days of ethical and spiritual soul-searching leading up to Yom Kippur, the Day of Atonement, the purpose of the secular New Year's Eve and New Year's Day is to party and have fun. The Jewish New Year, though of course a celebration, is primarily a time for introspection. Moreover, the Jewish New Year's difference is apparent throughout the holiday, not just when Jews are at synagogue. A significant part of this difference can be attributed to the Jewish law forbidding the handling of money on holy days. If the handling of money were forbidden on the secular New Year, people would find it impossible to celebrate it. That the comparison is not between Jewish and non-Jewish but between religious and secular is evidenced by the different ways in which secular and religious Jews in Israel celebrate Rosh Ha-Shanah. To secular Israelis, Rosh Ha-Shanah is a Hebrew January 1: a national holiday for travel, parties, and fun.

Jewish law gives us the possibility of bringing an aspect of holiness to the seemingly trivial events of our lives; or, more poetically, in the words of Abraham J. Heschel, "It gives us the opportunity to perceive the infinite even as we are performing the finite."

Morality vs. holiness. One final note: It is common to confuse morality and holiness. They are not the same, however, and the confusion between them hinders the achievement of both. An act may be unholy, or contrary to Jewish laws of holiness, without necessarily being immoral—for instance, "eating like a pig." Of course, the converse is not true: an immoral act, such as murder, is always an unholy act as well. It is therefore possible to act morally but be unholy, but it is not possible to act immorally and yet be holy. Judaism's laws of ethics must therefore be considered its most important, and taught accordingly.* The laws of holiness are of the utmost significance and are essential to Jewish life, but as Isaiah said, "The holy God is made holy through righteousness [not holiness]" (*Isaiah* 5:16).

NATIONAL LAWS

The final category of Jewish law is national. The Jewish people, like all peoples, has distinctive practices through which its members identify with the nation and commemorate events in its history.

Among the best known of Judaism's national laws is the eating of *matzah* during Passover. When the Jews were liberated from their slavery in Egypt, they did not have sufficient time to bake bread, and instead ate unleavened bread, *matzah*. Thirty-two hundred years later we still refrain from bread during the holiday that commemorates the Jews' exodus from Egypt. Likewise, Jews eat bitter herbs at the Passover Seder (the special Passover feast), so as to identify with the Jews who suffered enslavement in Egypt. The Passover Seder itself is largely a national *mitzvah*—which helps to explain why it is the most widely observed Jewish ritual among secular Jews.

Another national law legislates fasting on the Ninth of

---

* When the laws of holiness are emphasized more than the laws of ethics, we produce Jews who try to be holy before they are ethical. This is the problem of unethical seemingly religious Jews, discussed in Question 3.

Av, the national day of mourning for the destruction of the two Jewish states and the holy temples in 586 B.C.E. and 70 C.E. respectively. On a happier note are the holidays of Chanukah and Purim, both of which celebrate victories of the Jewish nation over her oppressors.

Most Jewish national holidays commemorate events of the distant past, but there are two holidays occasioned by events of this century—Yom Ha-Atzmaut, occurring on the fifth of Iyar (in May), which celebrates the establishment of Israel in 1948, and Yom Ha-Shoah, occurring on the twenty-seventh of Nissan (in April), which is Holocaust Remembrance Day.

While most Jewish laws fit neatly into one or two of the Jewish law categories, two extremely important institutions within Judaism, Shabbat and Kashrut, contain laws that fall into all four categories.

SHABBAT
The Shabbat is one of Judaism's unique contributions to civilization. Its observance is commanded in the Fourth of the Ten Commandments, testifying to its significance in the eyes of Judaism. The Shabbat and its many laws constitute Judaism's attempt to create on one day each week a taste of the Messianic Age.

In order to understand the Shabbat, it is first necessary to acknowledge that the purpose of Shabbat is to make each seventh day holy (*Exodus* 20:8); it is not to have us rest. If the purpose were to rest, then one who sleeps from Friday evening to Saturday night should be considered as having observed the Shabbat. Rest is only a byproduct of the Shabbat.

To achieve the purpose of Shabbat, one must observe

the Shabbat laws. Through observance of the Shabbat laws, the Shabbat day becomes a day of peace on earth.

PEACE WITHIN OURSELVES

One purpose of the Shabbat laws is to produce a state of inner peace by having us desist from all work not geared to making the Shabbat holy and by having us rely on our own minds and bodies. To achieve this state, the Shabbat laws' intent is to inhibit non-Shabbat work and the use of external sources of energy; in addition to its general prohibition of work, its prohibitions include the use of radio, television, and other machinery.

By not watching television, using machinery, or otherwise relying on external sources of creativity, people are compelled to return to themselves for creativity. All creativity on the Shabbat should come from within the human being, not from external sources and not from technology. Thus, for example, one should read but not write. Writing is forbidden because of its reliance upon an external vehicle for creativity, a pen or pencil. When writing, one relies upon the writing implement to create new words, but when reading, all creativity is within a person (his or her mind), since the words have already been created.

All week we rely upon, and often become enslaved to, external vehicles of creativity, amusement, and so forth, especially in the form of technology. On the Shabbat, however, we must return to ourselves and be liberated from dependence upon technology. While most modern men and women cannot conceive of life without cars, television, or telephones, one who observes the Shabbat revels in such a life. He or she spends one-seventh of his or her life (ten full years if he or she lives to be seventy) without relying on any of these things.*

The Shabbat also compels the individual to reflect on the most significant question concerning himself and technology. After spending six days at work, creating, utilizing and expanding technology, the individual is freed on the seventh day to reflect on the question: *Work and technology toward what purpose? For what did I work all week?*

PEACE BETWEEN PEOPLE

By ensuring that we refrain from reliance upon the inanimate, Shabbat laws compel us to seek relationships with the animate: first, ourselves, and then our family and friends. We who have experienced the Shabbat can testify to one nearly universal consequence of Shabbat observance: the strengthening of family unity and of friendships.

Those who observe Shabbat invariably do so with family and/or friends. The Shabbat laws, by prohibiting technological companionship, compel us to seek human companionship. The Shabbat meals are a typical example. The Friday night meal in a home which observes the Shabbat is a lengthy one at which all the participants sing and speak for hours on end. *Unlike the rest of the week, no one has another appointment to run to at the end of the meal.* If the talk is stopped to watch a basketball game, or to go to a movie, this means that

---

* Perhaps this idea will strike some as more palatable when put not in words of the Torah, but in the words of a contemporary and untraditional figure: Norman Mailer. During Mr. Mailer's campaign for mayor of New York in 1969, he suggested a radically new idea: Super-Sunday. On this day, Mailer suggested, traffic and transport should be minimized in the city, radio and TV should limit broadcasting, and peace would reign in New York City. Many found this idea to be another brilliant spin-off from a brilliant mind. Jews, however, have been observing Super-Saturdays for three thousand years.

basketball and movies are more significant than family discussion and Judaism.

When we speak about the effects of the lengthy Friday night meal on the family, people often react with envy and a feeling that in their families it would not work. They question whether their family would find enough to talk about for two or three hours, a question which is unfortunately a valid one for most people today. A common symptom of the contemporary breakdown of family life is the inability of members to communicate with one another on matters of any importance.* The Shabbat serves, therefore, not only as a day of reunion and elevation for a family, but also as a day that challenges a family to confront a question which many families prefer to avoid: Can the family members communicate with one another?

Parents and children relate better in a family that observes Shabbat, and as regards the husband-wife relationship, the benefits of Shabbat are profound.

PEACE BETWEEN PEOPLE AND NATURE

The Shabbat laws also ensure that people return to nature and not abuse it. To achieve this peaceful state with nature, the Shabbat laws' intent is to prevent any tampering with nature. *Both creation and destruction are prohibited on the Shabbat.*† As examples, one should not start a fire (therefore no smoking or cooking on Shabbat), or extinguish a fire which already exists (unless, of course, it is potentially de-

---

* One study done two years ago, for example, found that in the average home the husband and wife spend only 27½ minutes per week in discussion of issues unrelated to immediate family problems such as who needs the car or who will pick up the groceries.

† The conceiving of a child on Shabbat is not an exception to the ban on creating or destroying nature on Shabbat since it is creation *within us.*

structive), nor plant a tree (creation) or tear a leaf from a tree (destruction).

For one day each week specific Shabbat laws ensure that we do not rule over nature, just as other laws ensure that on this day we do not rule over fellow human beings or animals.

PEACE BETWEEN PEOPLE AND GOD

"The Shabbat," the Torah tells us, "is to God." All week we concern ourselves with what we want, but on Shabbat we reflect on what God wants of us. Shabbat is God's day. This is the ultimate Shabbat goal, because it can be attained only once we have begun to realize peace between ourselves and our fellow human beings, peace between ourselves and nature, and peace within ourselves. Only when we have started to achieve peace with this world are we free to transcend ourselves and approach God. This is accomplished in at least three ways: prayer and meditation, study of Torah, and sanctifying the day.

Life is composed of the material and the spiritual. During the week the material dominates. But Shabbat is a day on which matter is relegated to the background and the spiritual brought to the foreground. During the Shabbat, twenty-five hours in which time, not space, is sanctified (to borrow an idea from A. J. Heschel), man is given an opportunity to relate to the One Who has no body and is composed of no matter.

KASHRUT

While Shabbat practice is usually ignored but seldom disparaged by modern Jews, a practice that is often both ignored and disparaged is Kashrut (keeping kosher). Ask most Jews why the dietary laws of Kashrut exist and you are likely to receive this authoritative reply: "It was a health measure. For example, pigs were forbidden to avoid trichinosis. But with modern health codes, we certainly don't need such measures today."*

Unfortunately, this common opinion is an example of the "law of ignorant opinions authoritatively stated," which posits that in politics and religion the less a person knows, the more authoritatively he speaks. Worse yet, this view of Kashrut is reflective of a greater error regarding Jewish law. It seems that many Jews are convinced that Jewish dietary law does not constitute an ethical code but is really a health code. They contend that Kashrut was instituted to prevent disease, the Shabbat to keep us rested, circumcision to prevent cervical cancer, and so forth.

As it happens, the laws of Kashrut fall into all four categories of Jewish law, and are saturated with ethical meaning. The major purposes of Kashrut are:

1. to limit the number of animals the Jew is permitted to kill and eat (reflexive and ethical);
2. to render the slaughter of the permitted animals as painless as possible (ethical);
3. to cause revulsion at the shedding of blood (reflexive and ethical);
4. to instill self-discipline in the Jew (reflexive);
5. to help sustain Judaism and the cohesion of the Jewish community (national); and
6. to raise the act of eating from an animal-like level (holiness).

---

* The assumption that Kashrut is a health measure raises an interesting question. How do the people who believe that the prohibition of eating pigs was intended to prevent trichinosis account for the Jews' anticipating physicians' knowledge of the negative effects of eating pig by thousands of years?

The earliest of Judaism's dietary laws is the ban on eating meat with blood in it. According to Berkeley professor Jacob Milgrom, "surprisingly, none of Israel's neighbors possessed this absolute and universally-binding blood prohibition. Blood is everywhere partaken of as food. . . . Man has a right to nourishment, not to life. Hence the blood, which is the symbol of life, must be drained, returned to the universe, to God."* The unique practice of draining blood from meat consumed by Jews has had over thousands of years a profoundly moral impact. It has helped produce an extraordinary antipathy to bloodthirst. One example, in addition to the uniquely low incidence of violence among Jews, has been the virtual nonexistence of hunting for sport among Jews.

On the basis of this law, Judaism enacted another dietary law to protect animals from human cruelty, the ban on eating a limb from a living animal. This had been a common practice, but Judaism not only prohibited Jews from engaging in it, it made this prohibition one of the seven moral laws of the children of Noah to which all mankind is bound.

The next expression of Judaism's application of morality to eating animals constitutes the essential moral meaning of Kashrut. Keeping kosher is Judaism's compromise with its ideal of vegetarianism. Ideally, according to Judaism, man would confine his eating to fruits and vegetables, and not kill animals for food. In the Garden of Eden, Judaism's depiction of utopia, man was commanded to be vegetarian (*Genesis* 1:28–29). The future Kingdom of God on earth is also depicted as one in which all creatures will be vegetarian (*Isaiah* ll:7f). However, Judaism did not legislate its vegetarian ideal. There are two probable reasons: A vegetarian diet was nu-

* "The Biblical Diet Laws as an Ethical System," *Interpretation,* July 1963.

tritionally difficult, if not impossible, and in any case it would not have been observed, since meat-eating was an innate desire. Jewish law did not completely ban meat-eating, but severely restricted it and made it more humane. The Torah refers negatively to meat-eating as a "craving" to which concessions must be made (*Deuteronomy* 12:20). On the basis of this verse, the Talmud states, "The Torah teaches a lesson in moral conduct, that man shall not eat meat unless he has a special craving for it" (*Hulin* 84a; *Sanhedrin* 59b also discusses Judaism's vegetarian ideal).

The Jewish ideal is that we not kill for food. Its compromise, known as Kashrut, places a strict limit on the number of animal species which Jews may kill to eat, and legislates a uniquely humane manner in which to kill the permitted animals. The Jewish people is not permitted to kill every animal its members want to eat. This is one reason why the Torah mentions the word *holy* every time it mentions Kashrut.

The animals that are permitted, or kosher, to Jews to eat are identified by certain characteristics. A land animal must chew its cud and have "split" hooves, a fish must have both fins and scales, and a bird must not be a bird of prey. Since these characteristics alone determine which animals are kosher, one cannot speak of a Jewish "taboo" on pigs or any other particular animal. Pig is nonkosher solely because it does not chew its cud, not because it is "dirty" or for any other reason. To underscore this point, a medieval commentator on the Torah, the *Or Hachayim*, wrote that "the pig is named *chazir* because one day God will return (*yachzir*) the pig to being permitted[!]" (commentary on *Leviticus* 11:14).

But why these particular characteristics? Why couldn't it as easily have been the other way around? The answer may be given in the form of another question. If the characteristics of the kosher animals were reversed or altogether different, would we not ask the same question? Why land animals must chew their cud and have split hooves is a fascinating question, but it is irrelevant to Kashrut's moral purpose of limiting our killing and eating of animals. It is analogous to asking why red lights signify "stop" and green lights mean "go." There may be psychological or other reasons for the choice of these colors, but they are irrelevant to the primary purpose of traffic lights, which is to guide traffic. Red and green may have been selected arbitrarily. Similarly, the signs of kosher animals may be regarded as having been arbitrarily selected. Whether or not there are reasons for these signs no more determines the need for the system of Kashrut than whether or not there are reasons for green and red determines the need for traffic signals. Given Judaism's goal of limiting the number of animals Jews could kill to eat, some signs delineating kosher and nonpermitted animals had to be selected.*

The next step in Judaism's moral concern about eating animals was the requirement that the killing of the kosher animals be as painless and humane as possible. The moral premise behind the Jewish slaughtering regulations is that any wounded animal is automatically nonkosher. This legislation ensured that animals be killed as quickly and painlessly as possible *with one cut*. In addition, the *shochet* (slaughterer) could not be just any Jew—he had to be particularly pious and educated (since such a person would presumably be most

---

* Note this explanation from Philo, the first-century Jewish philosopher: The Bible probably believed that what people eat influences their behavior. The Torah, therefore, prohibited the Jews from consuming animals that kill and eat other animals so that we do not ingest a killer instinct. It is not a coincidence that every kosher animal is herbivorous, and that every carnivorous animal is nonkosher.

62

careful to minimize the animal's suffering); and an animal slaughtered with a dull, blunted knife is not kosher.

Thus the laws that put half of the animal world off limits to Jewish tables in conjunction with the myriad laws ensuring humane slaughter of the permitted half make up the systematic ethics of Judaism with regard to food.*

In addition, Jewish dietary law demands that we not eat milk or milk products and meat together. Based upon the thrice-mentioned biblical law, "Do not seethe a kid in its mother's milk," the oral legal tradition prohibited the eating of milk and meat together.

The intent of the original Torah law is obviously ethical, but what is the reason for separating milk and meat as a general rule? This concept is directly related to Judaism's obsession with separating death from life. Judaism is uniquely preoccupied with this life.

In ancient Egypt, out of which Judaism arose, the culture revolved around death; its bible was *The Book of the Dead*, and its priests were concerned with the dead. Apparently

---

* Kashrut may be regarded as but one part of Judaism's systematic ethics concerning the treatment of animals. Under the heading *tzaar ba'alei chayyim* (prevention of cruelty to animals) the Torah legislated over three thousand years ago that (1) just as you rest on the Shabbat, so must your animal rest (*Exodus* 20:10); (2) "you shall not plow with an ox and mule harnessed together" (*Deuteronomy* 22:10), since being of unequal size and strength both animals would suffer; (3) if a man comes across a nest of birds, he cannot slaughter the mother bird with the young, but must send the mother bird away to spare her feelings (*Deuteronomy* 22:6), for as Maimonides has written, "the pain of the animals under such circumstances is very great" (*Guide to the Perplexed* 3:48); (4) while treading out the corn, the ox (or any other animal) cannot be muzzled (*Deuteronomy* 25:4) so that while working in the field the animal will be free to eat as much as it desires. Later in the Talmudic period, the rabbis legislated that it is forbidden for one to eat in the morning before he has fed his animals (*Talmud Berakhot* 40a) or to purchase an animal if he is not sure that he can provide sufficient food for it.

this is why a *cohen*, or Jewish priest, cannot come into contact with a dead body; he must concern himself only with life.

Judaism asks us to separate meat (death) from milk (life). One proof of this explanation is that only milk-producing animals may not be eaten with milk. We are allowed to eat fish and milk together because fish do not produce milk. Milk does not represent life with regard to fish, as it does with regard to mammals.*

Kashrut, like all Jewish laws, also serves the crucial purpose of strengthening each Jew's self-control. In a famous passage in *Midrash Tanhuma Shmini* 7 (written about fifteen hundred years ago), Rav states that "the *mitzvot* [commandments—in this instance Kashrut] were given solely in order to train people. For what does it matter to the Blessed Holy one . . . about the 'purity' or 'impurity' of the animals we eat? It is clear, then, that the *mitzvot* were given solely for the purpose of training people."

The question is often posed: Is Kashrut really related to ethics or holiness—after all, it's not what goes into a man's mouth but what comes out that makes him impure (echoing Jesus in *Mark* 7:19)?

We would answer: *Every time a Jew sits down to eat a kosher meal he or she is reminded that the animal being eaten is a creature of God, that the death of such a creature cannot be taken lightly, that hunting for sport is forbidden, that we cannot treat any living thing irresponsibly, and that we are responsible for what happens to other beings (human and animal) even if we did not personally come into contact with*

---

* Chickens, which also do not produce milk, apparently were not originally considered "meat," as the Talmud itself noted that one of the great Talmudic rabbis, Rabbi Yosi Ha-G'lili, ate chicken with milk. As the tradition grew, however, it came to include chicken as "meat."

64

them. As an example of the latter concern, a Boston rabbinic court declared grapes picked by oppressed Chicano workers nonkosher; and perhaps we may similarly declare the skins of baby seals that were clubbed to death nonkosher to be worn.

Richard Israel has noted, "The observance of Kashrut is an example of an annoying series of *mitzvot* which I am glad not to have dropped because of some of the rather important surprises it has offered. Because it is a public observance, I have to justify it rather frequently, to my friends and certainly to myself. I find that whether I like it or not, Kashrut brings me into contact with a series of rather important questions: What is my responsibility to the calf that I eat . . . ? Is the earth and the fullness thereof mine to do with as I will? What does it mean that a table should be an altar? Is eating indeed a devotional act? . . . If Kashrut makes me ask enough questions, often enough, I discover that its very provocative quality is one of its chief virtues for my religious life."* †

---

* In Himmelfarb, ed., *The Condition of Jewish Belief,* p. 100.

† Aside from the important moral and social ideals communicated by the laws of Kashrut, there is yet one more effect which must be noted—the relationship of Kashrut to the social cohesion of the Jewish community. When a nonobservant Jew or non-Jew travels to a city where he has no acquaintances, he often remains there without ever coming to know the inhabitants. But when we travel, our observance of Kashrut immediately ensures that we meet local people. Usually we call the rabbi to inquire where kosher food can be obtained and more often than not an inquiry of this sort results in a dinner invitation, either to the house of the rabbi or to the home of a layman he might suggest. This has been our experience throughout the United States and on five continents. Later we go to synagogue where we meet other Jews and befriend new people. Because we share a value system and a lifestyle, there is instantaneous rapport between us. When Kashrut is observed, no Jew is ever alone in a city where there are other Jews.

Question 3

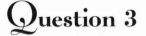

IF JUDAISM IS SUPPOSED TO MAKE PEOPLE BETTER, HOW DO YOU ACCOUNT FOR UNETHICAL RELIGIOUS JEWS AND FOR ETHICAL PEOPLE WHO ARE NOT RELIGIOUS?

The Torah is to the soul of man what rain is to the soil; rain makes any seed put into the soil grow, producing nourishing as well as poisonous plants. The Torah also helps him who is striving for self-perfection, while it increases the impurity of heart of those that remain uncultivated.

> —ELIJAH, THE GAON OF VILNA, IN HIS COMMENTARY ON *Proverbs* 24:31 and 25:4

. . . How is one to account for the goodness of so many irreligionists? Very simply. Men often behave better than their philosophies. They cannot be expected to persist in doing so. In the end, how a man thinks must affect how he acts: atheism must finally, if not in one generation, then in several, remake the conduct of atheists in the light of its own logic.

> —MILTON STEINBERG, *Anatomy of Faith*

65

HOW DO YOU ACCOUNT
FOR RELIGIOUS JEWS WHO
ARE UNETHICAL?

A problem that disturbs every sensitive Jew is the existence of Jews who observe many Jewish laws but who are, nevertheless, unethical people. This is a crucial problem because it is the existence of such people that often serves to invalidate religion in the eyes of others, and to make it easy to dismiss religion as mechanical rituals and hypocrisy.

"RELIGIOUS" MEANS ETHICAL

The premise of the question is in error, for a *Jew is not "religious" if he or she does not observe the Jewish laws of ethics and goodness.* To anyone familiar with Judaism this statement is as obviously true as the statement that a citizen of the United States is not considered law-abiding if he violates half of the American legal code. We feel compelled to state this, however, because of the unfortunate fact that religion is so often associated in people's minds solely with acts between people and God.

The laws between people and God, however, are but one part of Judaism (and even these, when performed with the proper intent, have profound ethical implications). Vast quantities of Jewish law and religious literature are concerned solely with actions between one individual and another, and these laws are as binding as Kashrut, *tefillin* (phylacteries), and prayer. There are general ethical rules, such as "Love your neighbor as yourself" (*Leviticus* 19:18), and there are innu-

66

merable specific and subtle ethical laws, as for example, the laws of charity, against gossiping, of proper business behavior, and the previously cited law which forbids a Jew to inquire of a storekeeper the price of an item, if he has no real interest in buying it (*Mishnah Bava Metziah* 4:10).

Judaism is so concerned with knowledge of, and precision in, ethics that it declares that "an ignorant person [i.e., one ignorant of the law] cannot be righteous" (*Mishnah Avot* 2:5). One who is observant of person-to-God laws but negligent in observing the ethical, or person-to-person, laws cannot be considered an observant or religious Jew. To call such a person religious is a contradiction in terms, for he is violating vast portions of Jewish law. The highest religious appellation in Judaism is *hasid*, which means one who practices righteous and kindly deeds.

The following ethical laws are taken from but nine verses (10–18) in *Leviticus* 19. *Is a Jew who violates these Torah laws religious or observant?*

1. To give charity to the poor and to the stranger;
2. not to cheat or mislead people;
3. not to oppress a worker by not paying him promptly;
4. that a judge not favor the rich (out of respect) or the poor (out of sympathy), but always dispense justice;
5. not to gossip;
6. not to stand by while another's blood is shed;
7. not to take revenge or even to bear a grudge; and
8. to show love to one's neighbor as to oneself.

Obviously, an unethical Jew is neither observant nor religious, and we fervently hope that these Jews who observe some of Judaism's laws while remaining unethical will either come to understand that God rejects the observance of person-to-God laws by people who act immorally, and thereafter carefully observe Judaism's moral laws; or stop pretending to be observant, religious Jews.

Unethical and unkind people who pretend to be religious commit the sin of *khillul ha-Shem*, the desecration of God's name. The consequent alienation from religion of people who might otherwise become or remain religious is underscored in the Talmud: ". . . If someone studies Bible and Mishnah [the Oral Law] . . . but is dishonest in business and discourteous in his relations with people, what do people say about him? 'Woe unto him who studies the Torah. . . . This man studied the Torah; look how corrupt are his deeds, how ugly his ways' " (*Yoma* 86a).

OBSERVANCE AND MORAL INTENT

Observance of Jewish laws between people and God does not render one more moral unless these laws are observed with the intention of becoming more moral. To expect otherwise, to expect that mechanical observance of Jewish person-to-God laws will automatically create moral individuals, is to confer upon Jewish law some magical quality which one would deem absurd if applied to any other area of life. Can one be expected to grasp the meaning of Shakespeare by mechanically reading his words without intending to learn from them? Is it not possible to read Shakespeare's plays and to learn little or nothing from them? Is Shakespeare then to be considered worthless?

This relationship between observance and moral intent is in no way a new interpretation of how Jewish law functions. The Bible consistently warns that the person-to-God laws can have but a minimal moral effect when observed without the intention of becoming moral. The Prophets vehemently attacked those Jews whose mechanical observance of these laws betrayed a lack of concern for the ethical principles underlying them (see, for example, *Jeremiah* 7).

The Jew who observes Jewish person-to-God laws while behaving in a reprehensible manner towards people treats these laws as exercises in ritual rather than as moral training. The result is observance which is morally, hence religiously, worthless.

ETHICAL EXCELLENCE

Having said these things about unethical seemingly observant Jews, we wish to add three points of perspective concerning observant Jews and ethics.

First, violent crime is virtually unknown among observant Jews, and this is as true in societies where Jews constitute the majority of the population (as, for example, in Israel) as where Jews constitute a minority. This abhorrence of bloodshed among Jews is historically attributable to Judaism and its laws. Kashrut, for example, has over the past three thousand years generated in Jews a reverence for all life. As French scholar Anatole Beaulieu wrote in 1895, "Consider the one circumstance that no Jewish mother ever killed a chicken with her own hand and you will understand why homicide is rarer among Jews than among any other human group."

Second, ethically excellent behavior is expected from observant Jews. Consequently, people are more likely to notice unethical and unkind acts committed by people considered to be religious. But it is well to bear in mind the observation of Elie Wiesel concerning the behavior of rabbis in the concentration camps. "In the camps, there were Capos [prisoners who worked for the Nazis] of German, Hungarian, Czech, Slovakian, Georgian, Ukranian, French and Lithuanian extraction. They were Christians, Jews and atheists. Former professors, industrialists, artists, merchants, workers, militants from the right and the left, philosophers and explorers of the soul, Marxists and staunch humanists. And, of course, a few common criminals. But not one Capo had been a rabbi."*

And third, the possibility of improving the ethical conduct of religious Jews is greater than the possibility of doing so among secular Jews. Among observant Jews there exists a recognized religious/legal code to which one can appeal if one wishes to improve their ethical conduct. Though they may violate this code, at least they recognize it as binding.

This was demonstrated during the Musar (moral) Movement within religious Jewish life in the nineteenth century. The following incident in the life of Rabbi Israel Salanter, the founder of the Musar Movement, illustrates how the ethical behavior of observant Jews may be improved by an appeal to the moral authority of the Torah.

During the reign of Czar Nicholas I, Jewish communities were forced to provide the Russian army with young Jewish boys for twenty-five year terms of service. Jewish communities consequently passed regulations to ensure that as long as there was a family from which no children had been taken, they would not conscript a second child from any family. Once, when visiting a city, Rabbi Salanter met a poor widow who was sobbing bitterly. When asked to explain her sorrow, she told the rabbi that she had just been informed that her second son was to be drafted because of the illegal intervention of a wealthy leader of the community

---

* *One Generation After* (New York: Random House, 1970), p. 189.

who wished to ensure that none of his children be taken. The rest of the community had acquiesced and decided to draft the widow's second child instead.

Salanter went that afternoon to the local synagogue, and when one man rose to lead the prayer service, the rabbi yelled at him, "It is forbidden for you to lead us in prayer for you are not a believer in God and Torah." A replacement was sent and Salanter shouted the same thing at the second man. This happened a third time. Finally, the congregants asked Rabbi Israel to explain his behavior. "The fact that you pray does not prove that you are believers," he answered. "You pray because your fathers prayed. But you are obviously not believers in the Torah. How do I know this? If you believed in the Torah, sincerely believing that it was the voice of God commanding you, then how would you dare ignore Torah laws which forbid you to oppress a widow, or to favor prominent people in a judgment? That you are willing to ignore such laws shows that you do not really believe in God and His Torah."

In order to improve the ethical behavior of religious Jews, Rabbi Salanter was able to appeal to their belief in the Torah.

What is urgently needed today is a renewed commitment among religious Jews, and particularly among their leaders, to ethical excellence. The religious Jew must serve as a moral light to secular Jews just as all Jews must serve as a moral example to the non-Jewish world. Imagine the effect it would have upon secular Jews if religious Jews were as identifiable by their commitment to ethical behavior as they are by their observance of Shabbat and Kashrut.

Many in the religious community are to blame for the widespread impression that religious Jews are no more ethical or kind than others. Too often the religious leadership and its followers have lent credibility to this impression by emphasizing observance of person-to-God laws far more than observance of person-to-person laws. As a result, when we speak of a "religious Jew," we immediately assume he or she keeps kosher and prays, but we do not necessarily assume that he or she is ethical.

A number of reasons can be suggested to explain this sad development. One is that while the religious community has always maintained communal institutions regulating rituals (for example, rabbinic supervision of Kashrut), it has had to allow governmental regulations to prevail in the more obviously social and ethical realms. Thus, one wishing to know whether a piece of meat is kosher will, of course, ask a rabbi, but if he wishes to know whether a given action is ethically kosher, he is far less likely to turn to his rabbi or to Jewish sources, despite the fact that ethical issues are comprehensively legislated in Jewish codes of law. Unfortunately, many religious people have come to view their limited Judaism as constituting all of Judaism, and restrict their religious concerns to the realm of the ritual.*

A second factor responsible for the fact that moral concerns are often not as great as they should be in the religious community is that Judaism is often transmitted to children not as a *moral* way of life but as nonrational habits which become a *social* way of life. Many children raised in observant environments come to observe Jewish laws not from

---

* It should be noted that there still are religious Jews who submit their business disputes to a rabbinic court, *Bet Din*, for adjudication. If both parties to the dispute agree to accept the ruling of the three rabbis, the decision will be upheld even in civil courts. My grandfather (J.T.), Rabbi Nissen Telushkin, of blessed memory, on a number of occasions sat as a rabbinical judge in cases involving many thousands of dollars.

an appreciation of the laws' moral and spiritual bases, but out of simple habit, out of fear of being "caught" violating a law, and because everyone around them is doing it. They are not taught to observe Jewish laws with the intention of becoming moral through them, and the laws, therefore, cease to have the morally elevating effect which they are meant to have.

The core of the problem is that much of the observant community has come to regard and to teach Jewish law as an end in itself, rather than as a means to "perfect the world under the rule of God." The term for the Jewish legal system, Halakha, means "way." Halakha is the "way" to reach a certain place, that place being morality and holiness. Too many Jews who travel the Halakha have forgotten that it is only a way and not the place to which it is supposed to lead. Whoever makes the way into an end is lost. "Sometimes," said the great hasidic rabbi Menachem Mendl of Kotzk, "a *mitzvah* [commandment] becomes idol worship [it, not God and goodness, becomes the end]."

HOW DO YOU ACCOUNT FOR ETHICAL PEOPLE WHO ARE NOT RELIGIOUS?

The ethics of an irreligious actively moral person stem from one or more of three factors: (1) the moral legacy of religion; (2) the individual's innate, or "natural," goodness; (3) a secular ethical philosophy (e.g., humanism).

THE MORAL LEGACY OF RELIGION
The foundations of morality in the West are religious. Though a moral individual may be irreligious, he acquired

his moral values from his ancestors who in all likelihood were religious, and/or from Western civilization which adheres (or at least pays lip service) to moral values formulated by Judaism and communicated by Christianity. The ethical secularist is essentially living by moral values inherited from thousands of years of religion.

Consequently, we ask whether the ethical secularist is capable of bequeathing a moral legacy to the next generation, now that he has cut them off from religion as the ultimate source of morality.* The answer, as history has shown, is no. The existence of righteous individual secularists notwithstanding, the legacy of ideologies which attempt to destroy religion has been unparalleled human suffering.†

---

* For a discussion of why a moral system is incoherent without God, see Question 1. The demise of morality which accompanies the demise of religion was powerfully described by Will Herberg: "The moral principles of Western civilization are, in fact, all derived from the tradition rooted in Scripture and have vital meaning only in the context of that tradition. The attempt made in recent decades by secularist thinkers to disengage these values from their religious context, in the assurance that they could live a life of their own as a 'humanistic' ethic, has resulted in what one writer has called our 'cut-flower culture.' Cut flowers retain their original beauty and fragrance, but only so long as they retain the vitality that they have drawn from their now severed roots; after that is exhausted, they wither and die. So with freedom, brotherhood, justice, and personal dignity—the values that form the moral foundation of our civilization. Without the life-giving power of the faith out of which they have sprung, they possess neither meaning nor vitality. Morality ungrounded in God is indeed a house built upon sand, unable to stand up against the vagaries of impulse and the brutal pressures of power and self-interest" (*Judaism and Modern Man*, New York: Atheneum, 1979; pp. 91–92).

† Auschwitz, the Gulag Archipelago, and Cambodia's Khmer Rouge are logical and probably inevitable outgrowths of atheism. In light of the unprecedented horrors of this century created by regimes which aim to destroy religion, the burden of proof is upon atheists to show that morality can survive the death of religion.

NATURAL GOODNESS: MORAL GENIUSES

A second explanation of the existence of ethical irreligious people is the simple fact that nature produces a certain number of naturally good people—moral geniuses, we may call them—just as it occasionally produces natural artists and scientific geniuses. But we cannot stop teaching music and rely on nature to occasionally blossom forth with musical geniuses. As music must be systematically taught in order to produce musicians, goodness must be systematically taught in order to produce good people.*

A SECULAR ETHICAL PHILOSOPHY

Finally, some ethical secularists will attribute their ethical values and behavior to a secular ethical philosophy, such as ethical humanism. We refer the reader to Question 4, wherein we compare Judaism and humanism at some length. Suffice it to say at this point that secular humanism is completely subjective, and has neither a God, nor a legal ethical code, nor a people, nor a mode of transmission from one generation to the next. Humanism has no system for producing good people. It is only a set of personal *ideals*, which in any case are usually only restatements of Jewish ideals. It is not surprising that the Ethical Culture Foundation was founded by a rabbi, Felix Adler, in 1876.

---

* The need for a systematized ethical system is illustrated by the experience of Andrei Sakharov, the Soviet physicist and winner of the Nobel Peace Prize, who devotes his life to the fight for human rights. Sakharov is that exceptional human being whose goodness can be characterized as "natural," rather than induced by any specific moral system. Yet having no such moral system, Sakharov has apparently been unable to pass his morality on to his children, all of whom support the Soviet police state, which oppresses their father.

CONCLUSION

In sum, the existence of actively moral irreligious individuals in no way negates the need for a moral system, for one based on religious principles, and for a community of adherents to that system. Even with the best intentions, ethical atheists cannot be relied upon to perpetuate ethics. As Milton Steinberg has written: " . . . How is one to account for the goodness of so many irreligionists? Very simply. Men often behave better than their philosophies. They cannot be expected to persist in doing so. In the end, how a man thinks must affect how he acts; atheism must finally, if not in one generation, then in several, remake the conduct of atheists in the light of its own logic."* It already has. The age of "me-ism" in our increasingly self-centered society is one such outgrowth of the secularization of our society. When the "something higher" embodied in God and religious values is destroyed, nothing is higher. In the secular age, we end up worshiping ourselves.

We therefore implore those secular individuals who are concerned with ethics and with fighting for a good world to reevaluate their secularism. Perhaps ethical monotheistic religion in general and Judaism in particular constitute better ways to achieve the incredibly difficult task of making better people and a better world.

----

* *Anatomy of Faith,* pp. 88–96.

Question 4

How Does Judaism Differ from Christianity, Marxism and Communism, and Humanism?

These three movements have three things in common. Each was founded by a Jew, each is a derivative of Judaism seeking to fulfill the messianic and utopian goals which Judaism introduced, but each changed the Jewish way of attaining these goals.

CHRISTIANITY

FAITH OVER WORKS

Whether or not Jesus was the Messiah is not the most important question that divides Judaism and Christianity. The major difference between Judaism and Christianity lies in the importance each religion attaches to faith and actions.* In Judaism, God considers people's actions to be more important than their faith;† acting in accordance with biblical and rabbinic law is the Jews' central obligation. As Christianity developed, however, it did away with most of these laws, and faith became its central demand.

Though faith became the essence of Christianity, Christian history reveals that this emphasis on faith over works was held by neither Jesus nor his immediate followers. The New Testament often notes that Jesus and his early followers stressed and observed Jewish law: "Do not imagine that I have come to abolish the Law or the Prophets," Jesus declared to his early disciples, "I tell you solemnly, till heaven and earth disappear, not one dot, not one little stroke, shall disappear from the Law [the Torah] until its purpose is

---

* The question of whether or not Jesus was the Messiah prophesied in the Bible—the issue with which most comparisons of Judaism and Christianity are concerned—is discussed later.

† This constitutes one of the few beliefs in Judaism that is affirmed across the Jewish religious spectrum, from the most Reform to the most Orthodox. In any synagogue, on any Shabbat or holiday, the emphasis in the rabbi's sermon is almost always on deeds. The nature of the deeds being emphasized might differ: in the Reform synagogue there might be greater emphasis on social action, and in the Orthodox, on the proper observance of the Shabbat, though increasingly it could be the other way around. But it is *inconceivable* that a rabbi would deliver a sermon on salvation through faith, a most common subject of Christian sermons.

achieved."* Jesus then concluded his message with a warning against anyone who violates Jewish law: "Therefore, the man who infringes even the least of these commandments and teaches others to do the same will be considered the least in the kingdom of heaven" (*Matthew* 5:17–19).

After his death, Jesus's disciples continued to heed their teacher's message to observe Halakha (Jewish law). *Acts* 2:46 and 3:1 state that the disciples regularly prayed at the Temple; *Acts* 10:14 records Peter's scrupulous observance of Kashrut (the Jewish dietary laws); *Acts* 15:1 teaches that "some men came down from Judea," (these men, in line with *Galatians* 2:12, appear to have been sent by James, Jesus's brother) to teach that "unless you have yourselves been circumcised in the tradition of Moses, you cannot be saved." In *Acts* 21:24, James says to Paul, ". . . let everyone know there is no truth in the reports they have heard about you, and that *you still regularly observe the Law.*"

However, in the year 70, when the Jewish community in Jerusalem was destroyed by the Romans, a new ideology regarding God's law became dominant in Christianity. The formulator of this new ideology was Paul of Tarsus, and he theorized as follows:

a. *all* the laws of the Torah must be observed—therefore breaking one of them renders one cursed: ". . . *scripture says: Cursed be everyone who does not persevere in observing everything prescribed in the book of the Law*" (*Galatians* 3:10);

b. man, being imperfect, will sin by violating a law: "*We*

---

* The law's purpose is, of course, the universal recognition of the rule of God, a goal which neither Christianity nor Judaism believes has been realized.

> could have been justified by the Law if the Law we
> were given had been capable of giving life, but it is
> not: scripture makes no exceptions when it says that
> sin is master everywhere . . ." (Galatians 3:21–2);
> c. man is cursed by the Law: ". . . those who rely on
> the keeping of the Law are under a curse . . ." (Gala-
> tians 3:10); and
> d. man must be redeemed from the Law, a redemption
> which can come only through belief in Jesus: "Christ
> redeemed us from the curse of the Law . . ." (Gala-
> tians 3:10). ". . . we conclude that a man is put right
> with God only through faith and not by doing what
> the law commands" (Romans 3:28).

Judaism's differences with this ideology are profound.
The Pauline idea that a person is cursed by God for breaking
any law (see Galatians 3:10–3) was a new one, not to be
found anywhere in the Bible or in normative Judaism. From
where, then, did Paul develop this notion? It appears from
Galatians 3:10 that he derived it from a mistaken reading of
a verse in the Bible, Deuteronomy 27:26. The eleven verses
before it, Deuteronomy 27:15–25, list eleven basic ethical
obligations (prohibitions against violence, bribery, idolatry,
incest, oppression of the defenseless, and so forth) and declare the transgressor of any of them cursed by the Jews and
Moses (not by God). At the conclusion of these verses the
Bible says, "Cursed be he who does not maintain all the words
of this Torah to do them . . ."—"this Torah [Teaching]"
referring to the eleven laws just listed. However, Paul understood this verse to mean, "Cursed be everyone who does not
persevere in observing everything prescribed in the book of
the Law" (as it is translated in Galatians 3:10). Paul misun-

derstood (or intentionally changed) the verse to mean that anyone who violates any law in the *entire* Torah (Five Books of Moses) is eternally cursed, a mistranslation which remains in the New Testament.*

The Bible appreciates that no human being can perfectly fulfill all its laws at all times, and it therefore understands that people will occasionally sin. Hundreds of years before Paul, the Jews were assured that God recognizes that "there is no man so righteous who does only good and never sins" (*Ecclesiastes* 7:20). Furthermore, the Bible repeatedly tells of Jews who sinned (including Moses and David) and who, after repenting and returning to observance of the law which they violated, were restored to God's grace, certainly without being eternally cursed.†

Needless to say, Judaism does not want people to violate its laws. But if a Jew does violate them, Jewish law enables him or her to return to God and right action through repentance—in Hebrew, *teshuvah*, from the word for "return."

---

* Anyone familiar with Hebrew will immediately perceive the mistranslation. But one need not know Hebrew to understand Paul's error; a simple reading of *Deuteronomy* 27:15–26 makes it clear, since, among other reasons, (a) there would have been no need to relist eleven commandments if *Deuteronomy* 26:26 referred to every law in the Torah, and (b) the Hebrew Bible frequently uses the words "Torah" and "this Torah" in reference to a specific group of laws (for the term "Torah," see *Leviticus* 6:2, 6:18, 7:37, 11:46, 13:59, 14:2, 15:32, and *Numbers* 6:21; for the expression "this Torah" see *Deuteronomy* 1:5, 4:8, 28:61; 31:9, 11).

† The notion of being eternally cursed by God raises two other new issues, hell and eternal damnation, concerning which it should be noted that *the word hell never appears in the Hebrew Bible, and eternal damnation is unknown to Judaism.* The Bible does speak of *sheol*, a Hebrew word which has been mistranslated as "hell," but this word means "grave." In *Genesis* 37:35, for example, Jacob speaks of going to *sheol*, his grave, without seeing Joseph. Jacob, the Patriarch, did not say he was going to hell. Also, the notion of a hell where sinners suffer eternally is foreign to Judaism and entered the Western world's religious consciousness through the New Testament.

Teshuvah consists of three steps: the sinner must recognize his sin, feel sincere remorse at having sinned, and resolve to return to fulfilling the law. There was also a fourth step during the time of the Temple—the bringing of a sacrifice—but since the destruction of the Temple this step has been unnecessary, *a fact long foreseen by the Bible.* In the words of Hosea (14:3), prophesying of a time when the Temple would no longer be standing, ". . . turn to the Lord, say to Him Forgive all iniquity and receive us graciously, *so we will offer the prayers of our lips instead of calves.*" Hosea's statement is paralleled by *Proverbs* 21:3, "To do righteousness and justice is more acceptable to God than sacrifices," and by the book of *Jonah,* which recounts that when the people of Nineveh repented, their sins were forgiven by God despite the fact that they brought no sin-offering.*

Finally, the doctrine that God would curse men whom He created imperfect for being imperfect is one which depicts God as cruel and sadistic,† notions utterly foreign to Judaism.

As noted at the outset, Judaism considers people's actions more important than their faith. The Talmud, basing itself on *Jeremiah* 16:11, stated: "Better that they [the Jews] abandon Me [God] and continue to observe My laws," because, the Talmud adds, through observance of the laws they will return to God (*Jerusalem Talmud, Hagiggah* 1:7).

Despite the Bible's emphasis on deed more than creed, Paul declared (*Romans* 3:28) that "we conclude that a man

---

* There are numerous other biblical passages referring to the possibility of forgiveness and redemption without sacrifices, e.g., *Leviticus* 26:40–5; *Deuteronomy* 4:29–31; *Jeremiah* 10–20; *Ezekiel* 22:15.

† This caricature of God which results from Paul's caricature of the law, is the major source of the pernicious myth which contrasts the "vengeful Jewish God of the Old Testament" with the "loving Christian God of the New Testament."

is put right with God only through faith and not by doing what the law commands."

Owing to the Pauline doctrine as formulated in *Romans*, the criterion by which Catholics came to judge people was faith plus sacraments; and the father of Protestantism, Martin Luther, differed from the Church not in stressing the supremacy of good deeds, but in stressing that faith alone, without sacraments, is sufficient. In *On Christian Liberty*, a pamphlet issued in 1520, Luther declared, "Above all things bear in mind what I have said, that faith alone without works, justifies, sets free and saves."

As a result, millions of Christians to this day believe that in God's eyes, a person's conduct is less important than his beliefs and many Christian clerics in the past accordingly persecuted people for their beliefs.

It may be objected that Christians who have committed evil acts have misconstrued Paul. Perhaps they have, for Paul certainly advocated loving behavior. The fact remains, however, that whereas in Judaism the good people of all nations attain salvation (*Tosefta Sanhedrin* 13:2), in Christianity, belief in Christ, not good deeds, had to become the sole means to salvation since, as Paul reasoned, *if good deeds could achieve salvation, there would be no purpose to the crucifixion and "Christ would have died in vain"* (*Galatians* 2:21).

CHRISTIAN DOGMAS AND JUDAISM

Three major dogmas distinguish Christianity from Judaism: original sin, the Second Coming, and atonement through Jesus's death. To Christians, these beliefs are needed to solve otherwise insoluble problems. For Jews, however, these beliefs are not needed because the problems do not exist.

1. CHRISTIAN PROBLEM: ORIGINAL SIN

Christian Solution: Acceptance of Christ through baptism.

Paul wrote: "Sin came into the world through one man. . . . Then as one man's trespass led to condemnation for all men, so one man's act of righteousness leads to acquittal and life for all men. For as by one man's disobedience many were made sinners, so by one man's obedience many will be made righteous" (*Romans* 5:12, 18–19). The baptismal solution was confirmed in the "Decrees of the Council of Trent" (1545–63): "Since the Fall caused loss of righteousness, thralldom to the devil and liability to the wrath of God, and since original sin is transmitted by generation and not by imitation, *therefore all which has the proper nature of sin, and all guilt of original sin is removed in baptism.*"*

In Judaism, original sin is not a problem. The notion that we are born sinners is not a Jewish one. Each person is born innocent. He or she makes his or her own moral choice to sin or not to sin.

2. CHRISTIAN PROBLEM: THE MESSIANIC PROPHECIES WERE NOT FULFILLED WHEN JESUS CAME

Christian Solution: The Second Coming.

For Christians a Second Coming is necessary so that Jesus can fulfill the messianic prophecies which he was supposed to have fulfilled during his lifetime. Jewishly speaking, this is not a problem since the Jews never had reason to believe that Jesus was the Messiah (see pp. 86–90). The solution is also untenable to Jews, since the Jewish Bible never mentioned a second coming.

---

* Cited in *Encyclopedia of Religion and Ethics* IX, p. 562.

3. CHRISTIAN PROBLEM: PEOPLE CANNOT ATTAIN
SALVATION THROUGH THEIR ACTIONS

Christian Solution: Jesus's death atones for the sins of those who have faith in him.

This problem does not exist for Judaism, since according to Judaism people *can* attain salvation through their actions.

In the solution to this problem, Christianity differs profoundly from Judaism. First, for what sins of mankind was Jesus's death supposed to atone? Since the Bible obliged only Jews to observe its man-to-God laws, the non-Jewish world could not have committed such sins. The only sins which non-Jews could have committed were against people. Does Jesus's death atone for people's sins against other people? Apparently so.

This doctrine directly opposes Judaism and its perception of moral culpability. According to Judaism, *God Himself* cannot forgive us for our sins against another person. Only the person or persons whom we have hurt can forgive us.

JESUS'S TEACHINGS AND JUDAISM

Since Jesus generally practiced Pharisaic (rabbinic) Judaism, most of his teachings parallel Jewish biblical and Pharisaic beliefs. There are, however, a number of innovative teachings attributed to Jesus in the New Testament—it is of course impossible to know whether these statements were actually uttered by him, or merely attributed to him—which differ from Judaism.

1. *Jesus forgives all sins:* "The Son of man has the authority to forgive sins" (*Matthew* 9:6). Even if one equates Jesus with God (itself a heretical notion to Judaism), this belief is a radical departure from Judaism. As already indicated, Judaism believes that God Himself does not forgive all

sins; He limits His power and forgives only those sins committed against Him alone. As the Mishnah teaches: "The Day of Atonement atones for sins against God, not for sins against man, unless the injured party has been appeased" (*Yoma* 8:9).

2. *Jesus's attitude toward evil people:* "Offer the wicked man no resistance. On the contrary, if anyone hits you on the right cheek, offer him the other as well" (*Matthew* 5:38-9) and "Love your enemies and pray for your persecutors" (*Matthew* 5:44). Judaism, in contrast, demands that the wicked man be offered powerful resistance. One of many such examples is the biblical approval of Moses's killing of the Egyptian slavemaster who was beating a Jewish slave (*Exodus* 2:12). A second example is the oft-repeated biblical injunction "you shall burn the evil out from your midst" (*Deuteronomy* 7:17). Similarly, Judaism does not demand that one love one's enemies—though it is completely untrue to claim as Matthew does that Judaism commands one to hate one's enemies (see *Matthew* 5:43)—but it does command that one act justly toward one's enemies. A Jew is not, for example, commanded to love a Nazi, as the statement in Matthew demands.*

3. *Jesus's claim that people can come to God only through him:* "No one knows the Father except the Son, and anyone to whom the Son chooses to reveal Him" (*Matthew*

---

* In stress situations, Jesus himself seems to have found it difficult to follow this principle (e.g., *Matthew* 10:32, 25:41), and virtually no Christian group has ever found it possible to utilize this principle in directing its behavior. Nor is this a moral ideal. One of the few Christian groups to incorporate "offer the wicked man no resistance" into its everyday life, the Jehovah's Witnesses, was used in the concentration camps as barbers by SS men confident that the Jehovah's Witnesses would do nothing to harm them or other Nazi mass murderers (see Evelyn Le Chene, *Mauthausen*, Fakenham, Norfolk, Great Britain: 1971, p. 130).

11:27), differs from the Jewish belief that everyone has direct access to God, for "God is near to all who call unto Him" (*Psalms* 145:18). The implication of the former statement, and to this day the belief of many Christians, is that only one who believes in Jesus Christ, i.e., a Christian, can come to God. Judaism holds that one can come to God without being a Jew.

WHY DO JEWS NOT ACCEPT JESUS AS THE MESSIAH?

Judaism does not believe that Jesus was the Messiah because he did not fulfill any messianic prophecies. The major prophecy concerning the messianic days is that "Nation shall not lift up sword against nation, nor shall they learn war anymore" (*Isaiah* 2:4; see also *Isaiah* 2:1–3, 11:1–10). World peace must accompany the Messiah, and should peace not come, the Messiah has obviously not come. The Talmud records that in the second century, Rabbi Akiva, the greatest rabbi of his age, believed that Simon Bar Kochva was the Messiah. Yet when Bar Kochva's revolt against the Romans was crushed, Rabbi Akiva recognized that Bar Kochva could not have been the Messiah (though he was still regarded as an essentially righteous man), because the Messiah, according to the Bible, will establish universal peace and enable the Jews to lead a peaceful and independent existence in Israel.

It has been obvious for over nineteen hundred years that the messianic days of peace have not arrived, yet Christians still contend that Jesus was the Messiah. What is the Christian explanation? There will be, according to Christians, a second coming, at which time Jesus will fulfill the messianic functions originally expected of him. For Jews, however, this explanation is logically unsatisfactory and the idea of a second coming is nowhere to be found in the Bible. In fact, it appears likely that this idea was not even known to Jesus himself, for he told his followers that some of them would still be alive when all the messianic prophecies would materialize (*Mark* 9:1; 13:30). This idea of a second coming was apparently formulated by later Christians to explain Jesus's failure to fulfill the messianic prophecies.

As for Christian attempts to cite the Jewish Bible to "prove" that Jesus was the messiah, David Berger, a scholar in the field and Associate Professor of History at the City University of New York, has written: ". . . we have overwhelming evidence that the Messiah has not come, and against this evidence we are confronted by a dubious collection of isolated verses, forcibly wrenched out of context and invariably misinterpreted."*

A common example of such misinterpretation is the translation and meaning which Christians have given to *Isaiah* 7:14, "Behold a young woman (*almah*) shall conceive. . . ." In *Matthew* 1:22–3, the verse was changed to read "a virgin shall conceive," and for nearly two thousand years this has been cited as "proof" that the virgin birth of Jesus was prophesied in the Bible. But *almah* does not mean virgin; the Hebrew word for virgin is *betulah* (see *Leviticus* 21:3; *Deuteronomy* 22:19; 23:28; and *Ezekiel* 44:22). Had Isaiah referred to a virgin he would have used *betulah*. The context in which the passage occurs also renders the Christological meaning untenable. The verses in Isaiah describe events that Ahaz (a king of Judah in the time of Isaiah) was expected to witness, seven hundred years before Jesus.

A second and more significant example of an attempt to

* Unpublished manuscript.

make a Jewish text Christian is the use of *Isaiah* 53 as a Christological reference. In this chapter Isaiah speaks of a suffering and despised "servant of God." The contention of some Christians that this refers to Jesus is purely a statement of faith. It has no logical basis in the biblical text. The "servant of God" is either the prophet himself who, like all the Jewish prophets, suffered for his service to God, or the people of Israel, who are specifically referred to as the "servant of God" nine times in the previous chapters of *Isaiah* (41:8,9; 44:1,2, 21, 26; 45:4; 48:20; 49:3). This Christianizing of such a significant Jewish concept led the Jewish philosopher Eliezer Berkovits to write: "God's chosen people is the suffering servant of God. The majestic fifty-third chapter of Isaiah is the description of Israel's martyrology through the centuries [and] the way Christianity treated Israel through the ages only made Isaiah's description fit Israel all the more tragically and truly. Generation after generation of Christians poured out their iniquities and inhumanity over the head of Israel, yet they 'esteemed him stricken, smitten of God, and afflicted.' "*

Fortunately, in recent years many Christian scholars have also acknowledged the illegitimacy of attempts to "prove" Jesus's messiahship from the Jewish Bible. J. C. Fenton, in his *The Gospel of St. Matthew,* wrote: "It is now seen that the Old Testament was not a collection of detailed forebodings of future events, which could only be understood centuries later: the Old Testament writers were in fact writing for their contemporaries in a way which could be understood by them, and describing things that would happen more or less in their own lifetime. Thus Matthew's use of the Old

* *Faith After the Holocaust* (New York: Ktav Publishing House, Inc., 1973) pp. 125–6.

Testament . . . is now a stumbling-block to the twentieth-century reader of his Gospel."* The distinguished Christian scholar and theologian W. C. Davies likewise noted that the Gospels quote the Jewish Bible selectively: "There were some prophecies which they ignore and others which they modify."† Another Christian scholar, R. Taylor, noted in his commentary on *Psalms* 16:8–10 in *The Interpreter's Bible* that the New Testament interpretation misreads the clear intention of the Psalmist.

In sum, to call anyone who does not actually bring about the messianic era the Messiah is untenable to the Jews. To equate anyone with God, as normative Christianity does, is to Jews more than untenable. It compromises their ideal of monotheism.

CONCLUSION
Though there are significant differences between Judaism and Christianity, these differences should not constitute an obstacle to the development of close relationships between Jews and Christians. Indeed, many Christians are in the forefront of the struggle for an ethical monotheistic world; and we share more values with them than with some of our fellow Jews. And as regards the differences between Judaism and Christianity, as Trude Weiss-Rosmarin has written: "The notion that Judaism and Christianity, to maintain harmonious relations, must be 'truly, basically one,' is really a totalitarian aberration. For democracy is predicated on the conviction that dissimilarities and differences are no cause or justification for inequality. . . . After all, we don't demand that all

---

* Baltimore: Westminster, 1963, p. 178.
† "Torah and Dogma—A Comment," *Harvard Theological Review*, April 1968, p. 99.

Americans vote for the same ticket in order to promote national unity."*

This last point is crucial. While we must not demand that all Americans vote for the same party, we do feel it legitimate to demand that all Americans feel committed to the democratic process. Once this appreciation for democracy is shared, there is room for disagreement. The same is true of religion. Just as we presuppose a commitment to the democratic process on the part of Republicans and Democrats, so we presuppose that Christians and Jews are committed to live by and advocate ethical monotheism.

We need more discussions today between Jews and Christians to formulate a program to "perfect the world under the rule of God." The Western world is sinking into secular moral relativism, materialism, and hedonism. Our dialogue must therefore be motivated not by a desire to convert each other, but by a desire to convert a secular amoral world into a religious moral one.

MARXISM AND COMMUNISM

> *Right can never be higher than the economic structure of society and the cultural development thereby determined. We therefore reject every attempt to impose on us any moral dogma whatsoever as an eternal, ultimate and forever immutable moral law. . . .*
> —KARL MARX, *Capital*

---

* *Judaism and Christianity—The Differences* (New York: Jonathan David, 1965), pp. 11–12.

We say that our morality is entirely subordinated to the interests of the class struggle of the proletariat. . . . We do not believe in an eternal morality. . . . We repudiate all morality derived from nonhuman [i.e., God] and nonclass concepts.
> —VLADIMIR ILYICH LENIN, Address to the Third Congress of The Russian Young Communist League, October 2, 1920

. . . for Marxism there is no reason (literally no reason: our universe, the movement posits, is the kind of universe where there cannot conceivably be any reason) for not killing or torturing or exploiting a human person if his liquidation or torture or slave labor will advance the historical process.
> —PROFESSOR WILFRED CANTWELL SMITH, *Islam in Modern History*

You shall do no unrighteousness in judgment; you shall not respect the person of the poor [worker], nor favor the powerful [capitalist] but in righteousness you shall judge your neighbor.
> —Leviticus 19:15

MOTIVATING AIMS

Marxism and Judaism are both motivated by the desire to perfect the world and establish a utopia on earth. It was Judaism that first brought the utopian and messianic vision to mankind: from God's promise to Abraham, the first Jew,

"Through you all the families of the earth will be blessed" (*Genesis* 12:3), to the Prophets' unique expressions of universal brotherhood and peace, such as Isaiah's call to nations to "beat their swords into plowshares."

Marxism is a secular offshoot of Judaism's mission to perfect the world. It is in this context that the messianism and utopianism of Karl Marx become explicable. The thinking of this grandson of two Orthodox rabbis was rooted in Judaism's preoccupation with morality. As the [non-Jewish] scholar Edmund Wilson wrote in his history of socialism: "The characteristic genius of the Jew has been especially a moral genius. . . . Nobody but a Jew [Marx] could have fought so uncompromisingly and obstinately for the victory of the dispossessed classes."*

Thus, it is not to their motivating aims that one must look to find the essential differences between Marxism and Judaism.

THE SYSTEM

This is the second area in which there are more similarities than differences between Marxism and Judaism. Both are all-encompassing world views. In fact, they may both be called religions.

Since it is not surprising that we would characterize Judaism as a religion (though it is not only that), let us explain our reference to Marxism as a religion.

To the believing Marxist, Marxism is a religion. It has its own gods (man and materialist progress), prophet (Marx), apostles (Lenin, Stalin, Mao), absolute (materialism), ethic (proletarian solidarity), utopian visions, all-embracing an-

---

* *To The Finland Station* (Garden City, New York: Anchor Double-day, 1953), p. 307.

swers, community of believers, traditions, schisms, and even churches (first Moscow and, since the Chinese Reformation, Beijing and other smaller churches). "The religious essence of Marxism is superficially obscured by Marx's rejection of the traditional religions. . . . Like medieval Christianity, Marx's system undertakes to provide an integrated, all-inclusive view of reality, an organization of all significant knowledge in an interconnected whole, a frame of reference within which all possible questions of importance are answered or answerable."*

Though Marxism and Judaism may have similar goals, and both are all-inclusive world views, they diametrically oppose one another in almost every other way.

THE HIGHEST BEING

Their most obvious difference concerns God and man. Whereas for Judaism "God is the Lord, there is none other," for Marx "the highest being for man is man himself."† Man is god, and conversely, as Engels wrote, "God is man."‡ Moreover, the Marxist man/god is a jealous god who tolerates no other gods; Marx wrote that "human self-consciousness . . . [is] the supreme divinity—by the side of which none other shall be held."§ As the Jewish God transcends man and also tolerates no other gods, the lines of battle between

---

* Robert Tucker, *Philosophy and Myth in Karl Marx* (Cambridge: Cambridge University Press, 1961), p. 22.

† Karl Marx, "Zur Kritik der Gegelschen Rechtphilosophie," in Marx and Engels *Der historische Materialismus; Die Fruhschriften,* (Leipzig: 1932, I), p. 272; cited in Alfred G. Meyer, *Marxism, The Unity and Theory of Practice* (Ann Arbor: University of Michigan Press, 1963), p. 51.

‡ Marx and Engels, *MEGA* (Historische-Kritische Gesamtausgabe) *II,* p. 428, cited in Tucker, *Philosophy and Myth in Karl Marx,* p. 73.

§ Marx and Engels, *MEGA I,* p. 10; cited in Tucker, *Philosophy and Myth in Karl Marx,* p. 74.

Marxism and Judaism would seem to be clearly drawn. But as we shall see, this difference is much less significant than its consequences.

MORALITY

Marxism denies the existence of God, and as we have seen in Question 1, when God is denied, morality is relative and therefore objectively nonexistent. Marxists from Marx to Lenin to Mao have agreed that morality is relative (to the class), that *all revolutionary behavior is morally justified*, and that to oppose such behavior on the grounds that morality transcends classes is to suffer from "bourgeois morality."

"Right can never be higher than the economic structure of society and the cultural development thereby determined," wrote Marx. "We therefore reject every attempt to impose on us any moral dogma whatsoever as an eternal, ultimate and forever immutable moral law on the pretext that the moral world too has its permanent principles which transcend history and the differences between nations. We maintain on the contrary that all former moral theories are the product, in the last analysis, of the economic stage which society had reached at that particular epoch."

To this Lenin added: "We say that our morality is entirely subordinated to the interests of the class struggle of the proletariat. . . . We do not believe in an eternal morality. . . . We repudiate all morality derived from nonhuman [i.e. God] and nonclass concepts."*

In no area of life is the total opposition of Marxism to Judaism so apparent as in morality. Marxist morality sanctions any act so long as that act was committed "in the

* Address to the Third Congress of the Russian Young Communist League, October 2, 1920.

interests of the class struggle." Consequently, the morality of any act is determined by whichever Marxist is in power. The line between Marx and the Gulag Archipelago is direct; dropping "class enemies" into vats of acid (see Aleksandr Solzhenitsyn, *The Gulag Archipelago*, New York: Harper and Row, 1974) is not an immoral act for Communists. By what Communist code of morality could such actions be morally condemned?

The Marxist denial of a universal morality must lead to the demise of political freedom and the ascent of tyranny. As Professor Henry Bamford Parkes has observed: "The doctrine that all ideals and all values are socially determined leads . . . to tyranny of the collectivity or of its embodiment in a dictator. Only the belief in objective rational truth and moral values can preserve freedom; for it is only through the right of appeal to objective standards that men can judge the actions of their government and resist them when they believe them to be wrong."*

Judaism, on the other hand, gave the world ethical monotheism, the objective moral values without which tyranny is inevitable. *Personal moral behavior is the essence of Judaism; it is irrelevant to Marxism.* The objection that Stalin was an aberration, or in the Marxist dialect a "deviationist," may be true in relation to his economic policies—but this argument is untenable in the area of morality. First, there is *nothing* in Marxism which would declare immoral Stalin's murder of eighteen million people whom he declared enemies of the working class. Only if one holds that morality transcends economic, national, and individual interests can such actions be declared immoral. But a morality "which transcends his-

---

* *Marxism: An Autopsy* (Chicago: University of Chicago Press, 1939), p. 177.

tory and the differences between nations" is precisely what Marxism rejects. Second, Stalin did not begin the use of terror for Marxist ends. He only expanded the terror that Lenin and other Marxists began. The one exception proves the rule: "In his *Left-wing Communism, an Infantile Disorder* (1920), Lenin condemned terrorism (e.g., political assassination) because the Bolsheviks held at the time that it weakened the proletarian movement by encouraging the masses to believe that the revolution could be won for them by a few 'heroic individuals' instead of carrying it out for themselves. But he was careful to point out that his objection was 'of course only based on considerations of expediency,' and Marxists have long since been permitted to use such methods if they are likely to be successful."* Third, during Stalin's lifetime, virtually all people who considered themselves Marxists continued to revere Stalin as a true Marxist.†

DETERMINANT OF MAN'S BEHAVIOR
Marxism holds that economics is the primary determinant of human history. Accordingly, one must look to economic forces to find the source of antisocial behavior. People commit evil acts as a direct consequence of their economic position.

Though Judaism is well aware of the importance of economics and society, and attempts to morally affect them, it holds that it is human nature that first determines people's actions. Greed in human nature may have helped create capitalism, but capitalism did not create greed in human nature.

---

* R.N. Carew Hunt, "The Ethics of Marxism" in Michael Curtis, ed., *Marxism* (New York: Atherton, 1970), pp. 109–110.

† To this day, this Hitler-like mass murder is still revered by the Chinese Communist government, which keeps his portrait on display in the main square of Beijing and continues to issue postage stamps in his honor.

People create society, and in an evil society, individuals are expected to rise above it. *People, not economic forces, built Auschwitz and the Gulag Archipelago.* It is to underscore this very point that the Bible begins with two morality tales. First it tells of the second two men in history, Cain and Abel, and portrays one of them as a murderer! One major point of this story is that evil comes from *within* the human being; no society existed which corrupted the second man in the world. Next, the Bible relates the tale of Noah, the one moral man in the world and therefore the only one spared by God in the flood. Every person in the world was held responsible for his or her unethical behavior despite the fact that the entire world, excluding Noah, was evil.

WAYS TO ACHIEVE PERFECTION

Since according to Marxism economics determines history and causes the evil therein, the existing economic order must be overthrown. Thus the Marxist must work to bring about revolution.

Judaism aims to solve the problem of an unjust world, but it rejects revolution as the solution since *the roots of evil and injustice lie not in economics or society but in man himself.* Consequently, Judaism is a system designed to change individuals before it and they can ever hope to succeed in perfecting the world. This is admittedly a considerably slower, hence less romantic, process than fomenting revolutions, and many people find its demands too restrictive compared with the personal moral anarchy of revolution-making. But Judaism's method is infinitely more effective in achieving its results, for when Marxist revolutionaries attain power they are at least as cruel as their predecessors. Why shouldn't they be? Do these "revolutionaries" have higher standards of morality? There is simply no reason to trust that such revolutions will achieve *moral* results since the people acceding to power are no better, and often worse, than those they replace. The descent from the idealistic theories of Marx to the unparalleled (except for Hitler) mass brutality of Lenin, Stalin, Mao, Brezhnev, Cambodia's Pol Pot, and other Marxists who attain power, should surprise no one. Such evil is inevitable in a system such as Marxism which lacks personal moral responsibility, and which holds that economic institutions, not people, must first be changed.

HUMAN NATURE

At this point it should be clear what position Judaism and Marxism hold concerning the nature of man. Since Marxism maintains that economic forces are primarily responsible for the evils that people commit, and since the Marxist solution to antisocial behavior is revolution, Marxism must proceed from the assumption that people are basically good. It could be no other way, for if Marx were to assume that people would do evil irrespective of their economic position, his theories would be worthless as a guide to perfecting the world.

To "scientifically" substantiate the thesis that human nature is naturally good, Engels wrote in 1884 *The Origins of the Family, Private Property and the State.* The book, based upon the now discredited writings of an American anthropologist, Lewis Morgan, purported to show that original man was really a wonderful fellow who became corrupt only with the advent of technology and property. Primitive man, according to this work, lived in a sort of ideal primitive communist society wherein cooperation and nonexploitation were the rules of life and mankind was one big happy family. Until the advent of property, classes, and "self-alienating labor," people lived in a state of goodness which can return only in a communist society. Then, no economic obstacle will prevent people from expressing their true nature, goodness.

Concerning man's innate goodness or lack of it, Judaism is quite explicit. Among the Torah's first descriptions of man is God's statement that "the predilection of man's heart [or mind] is evil from his youth" (*Genesis* 8:21).* This does not mean that Judaism believes man to be inherently evil, but since man is naturally selfish, not altruistic, it is easier to do evil than to do good. We must be taught goodness and discipline ourselves to do what is good. Man needs correctives in order to channel his id or productive powers creatively, for good rather than evil. "Man has a poison in him," says the Talmud, "and the Torah is the antidote" (*Kiddushin* 30b).

Marx lived during the era when people were drunk with optimism. The nineteenth-century Western liberal worshiped man, it was the age of Prometheus unbound. We who live after Freudian revelations, Auschwitz and the Gulag Archipelago, and daily reports of sadism and wanton cruelty, reject naive belief in the "noble savage." Modern man is inherently no different from primitive man. We all have the capacity to be Cain. Each person must struggle with moral weakness as if he or she were the first person on the earth.

Marxists hold that people are basically good. Yet, how good are people if all it takes is economics to drive them to commit evil? How do Marxists account for totally different ethical behavior among different people in the same economic class and circumstances? And, if we are basically good and economic factors beyond our control cause us to act in a cer-

---

* Man's creation "in the image of God" does not mean that man is basically good. It means that man, unlike animals but like God, has the knowledge of good and evil.

tain way, how do Marxists sanction hurting "class enemies" whose only fault is their having been born into the wrong class? The answer to all these questions is that for Marxism individuals have little importance. As G. D. H. Cole noted, for Marx "not individuals but only social classes possess ultimate reality."*

According to Judaism, man must first work upon himself to become good; according to Marxism, man starts out good and need not change himself, only society.

FREEDOM

Both Judaism and Marxism revolve to a large extent around their conceptions of freedom. Yet these conceptions differ profoundly.

For Marxism, which conceives of the world in materialist terms, bondage is defined solely as servitude to external sources such as slave owners, capitalist bosses, or other forms of materialist inequality. Freedom is liberation from such servitude; it is the workers' loss of their chains.

For Judaism, freedom plays a crucial role. Jewish history can be said to have begun with the Jews' liberation from Egypt, "the house of bondage," and the Shabbat, as well as Passover, is based on the theme of liberation. But Judaism sees people as equally enslaved by two forms of bondage, external and internal. Once liberation from external servitude takes place, one must then liberate oneself from internal domination, the domination of one's life by passions, needs, irrationality, and wants. This is why Judaism does not consider the ancient Jews to have been fully liberated even after

---

* *Capital*, Introduction, p. xxviii; cited in Tucker, *Philosophy and Myth in Karl Marx*, p. 221.

the exodus from Egypt; they were only externally free. Only with the receiving of the Law at Sinai could they embark on the difficult process of liberating themselves from internal masters and attaining full freedom: "A person is not free unless he involves himself in the Torah," according to the Talmud (*Ethics of the Fathers* 6:2).

In the well-chosen words of Princeton's Robert Tucker, *"the only problem freedom can solve is bondage;* otherwise it represents not a solution but merely an opportunity. The real . . . emergence of man . . . into adulthood, will only take place if this opportunity is realized and worthy solutions of the problem of human existence in freedom are found."*

Tucker's words precisely echo Judaism's view of freedom. Judaism is not content with external liberation. But this is not the Marxist view. All man needs, according to Marx, is external liberation, since "freedom . . . is the essence of man. . . . No man fights against freedom."† How, then, would Marx explain the massive "escape from freedom," to use the famous words of Erich Fromm, which has been expressed in twentieth-century man's attraction to totalitarianism? Marx never had to; he was living during the century of belief in man.

We know now, however, that those who believe that "the essence of man is freedom," and that he therefore needs no internal controls, have produced societies far less free than those who have understood that "the predilection of man's heart is evil from his youth" and who therefore emphasized the need for self-discipline and internal controls. Alexis de Tocqueville prophesied correctly: "He who seeks in Liber-

* Tucker, *Philosophy and Myth in Karl Marx*, p. 237; emphasis ours.
† "Debate on the Liberty of the Press," *Rheinische Zeitung*, 12 May 1842.

ation anything other than Liberty itself is destined for servitude."

So long as we continue to think of freedom solely as liberation from external evils and continue to ignore the necessity for internal controls, there is not the slightest chance that world or personal violence will diminish, or that freedom will increase.

Finally, one must question the entire Marxian notion of human freedom. If indeed people's behavior is determined by their class and economic circumstances, how free are we? If we are so helpless in the face of economic forces, are we really "free in essence"?

Just as, according to Judaism, people must work at making themselves good, so too must they work at making themselves free. Marxism sees no such need.

CONCLUSION

If Marxism were only an economic philosophy, there would be no need to contrast it with Judaism. Judaism has no quarrel with any economic system so long as it is moral. A good Jew can live in a capitalist society or in a socialist society (such as the kibbutzim in Israel).

But the Jewish conflict with Marxism and Communism is not economic, it is moral. Marxism is not just an economic view, it is an all-embracing "scientific," philosophical, moral, political world view. The ultimate issues are far greater than Marxism and Communism versus capitalism, but are matter versus transcendence, determinism versus freedom, relative morality* versus universal morality, and man's innate goodness versus man's potential goodness.

* "This growth of moral relativism is the most alarming tendency in both the theory and the political practice of the modern world. . . . By

The issues separating Judaism and Marxism are so great and numerous that we would characterize the ultimate battle in the contemporary world as one between Moses and Marx, between monotheism and totalitarianism.

HUMANISM

Reason is amoral, education is amoral, and human nature is amoral. Yet these constitute the basis of the secular humanist's prescription for a moral world.

Humanism appeals to many individuals who though despairing of God and organized religion, remain committed to the ideas of ethical behavior and making a better world. Humanism is based on the assumption that we do not need God or religion to make an ethical world.

Because we have dealt in detail with the issues of God and morality, the need for an organized religious-ethical system, and the reasons for ethical people who are not religious in Questions 1, 2, and 3, our discussion here will be brief. If the reader has not already done so, he should read those three answers first, the second part of Question 3 in particular.

Since both humanism and Judaism aim to create an ethical world, the most important question is: Which is more

---

interpreting all cultural phenomena in terms of class struggle, by explaining all the beliefs of every individual by his role in that struggle, by proclaiming that any means whatever are justified in achieving the end, and that the only predestined historic end is the conquest of power by the proletariat, Marxism subordinates man to the march of history and ennobles tyranny, dishonesty, cruelty, and mass murder" (Parkes, *Marxism: An Autopsy*, pp. 177–8).

likely to realize this aim, ethical humanism or ethical monotheism?

For the following reasons, most of which are developed elsewhere in this book, it would seem clear that Judaism would constitute the more effective ethical system.

Humanism holds either that morality is relative, in which case everyone is free to choose the definition of good and evil that he or she prefers, and morality is, therefore, nonexistent (see pages 21–25); or that there *are* moral absolutes, in which case the secular humanist has simply substituted his own moral absolutes for God-based moral absolutes.

Since it denies the existence of God, humanism derives its moral ideals from man. But from which man? The brightest? The most rational? The leader? The majority?

The humanist answers that "moral values derive their source from human experience."* But who is to interpret the human experience for all of us? Or is everyone to interpret it for himself? Humanists usually argue that the latter is the case. But then we are back to moral relativism and no universal standard of morality.

To this the humanist responds that *reason* will establish morality. Reason is the humanists' arbiter of good and evil; it is for many humanists their religion: "rationality, or the attempt at it," writes Brand Blanshard, Professor of Philosophy at Yale, "takes the place of faith. . . . Take reason seriously. . . . Let it shape belief and conduct freely. It will shape them aright if anything can."†

As we have seen (pages 23–24), the belief that reason leads to moral behavior is itself irrational. Reason is amoral. It

---

* *Humanist Manifesto II*, issued in 1973.
† *The Humanist*, November–December 1974.

can be used to justify any morality and any crime.* As noted in Question 1, "The use of reason to justify what is wrong is so common that we have a special word for it—rationalization." In addition, reason often conflicts with morality since morality often demands conduct which opposes reasonable self-interest. Though it was the *moral* thing to do, few people in Nazi-occupied Europe found it *reasonable* to oppose Nazi atrocities—and those who did obeyed morality, not reason.

In addition to reason, humanists place great faith in secular education as leading to a good society. As Sigmund Freud wrote in Vienna in 1927: "Civilization has little to fear from educated people and brain-workers. In them the replacement of religious motives for civilized behavior by other, secular motives, would proceed unobtrusively. . . ."†

As Dr. Freud was to witness within ten years of his statement, civilization has as much to fear from educated people as from the uneducated. Freud's fellow Austrian and German intellectuals showed no more moral insight or strength than any other group of Germans and Austrians. Many of them not only supported Nazism but, as indicated by the record of the German Medical Association and the evidence cited in Max Weinreich's *Hitler's Professors,*‡ also participated in its atrocities.

Nor did many intellectuals in the democracies exhibit moral acuity. As regards Western intellectual support of Stalin, for example, Professor George Watson of Cambridge University has written: "The published evidence alone demon-

* To reasonable men of ancient Greece, reason dictated that unhealthy babies be left unattended to die. In the twentieth century, many thought it reasonable to support Fascism or Communism.

† *The Future of an Illusion* (New York: Norton, 1961), p. 39.

‡ New York: YIVO, 1946.

strates that many Western intellectuals in the age of Stalin believed in extermination in the sense of wanting it to happen."*

There is rarely a relationship between secular education and moral behavior. Just as reason is an amoral tool, as easily used for evil as for good, so, too, education is an amoral tool.

We therefore again ask the humanist, upon whom or what can we rely to decide morality once the religious basis of ethics is destroyed?

The third pillar of humanism, along with reason and education, is the belief that people are basically good. Humanists believe in humans.

Given the massive cruelty of human history, and particularly the butchery of this century, not coincidentally the most irreligious in history, the humanist's faith in the innate goodness of people must be deemed considerably more irrational than the Jew's faith in God and the *potential* goodness of people. One can only marvel at the secular humanists' belief in people's intrinsic goodness. No amount of slaughter, war, rape, crime, cheating, or apathy to evil shakes their belief that people are basically good. The popularity of violence in films, the throngs who cheer at hockey fights, and the cruelty of children toward weaker peers do not even dent the humanists' faith in humanity.

Reason is amoral, education is amoral, and human nature is amoral. Yet these constitute the basis of the secular humanist's prescription for a moral world.

Humanism speaks of few ethical ideals which Judaism has not advocated for the last 3,200 years and succeeded to an impressive extent in inculcating at least in the Jewish

---

* "Were the Intellectuals Duped?" *Encounter*, December 1973.

people. And Judaism offers at least four things which humanism lacks for realizing its ethical ideals:

1. A *system of ethical laws*. Judaism contains the most
   extensive ethical system known to mankind—see Question 2 for a description of this system. Does humanism
   have systematic laws on charity binding on all people
   born to humanist parents (as Judaism has—see appendix)? Is there a two-hundred-page humanist volume on gossiping (as Judaism has—see p. 48)? Is there
   any humanist code of laws geared to implementing
   its proclaimed ethics? The answer to these questions
   is no. Humanism has ideals but no legal system of
   implementation.
2. A *system of ethical laws based on God*. Judaism does
   not *suggest* to its adherents that they act kindly to fellow human beings, honestly in business, or with compassion to animals; it *commands* Jews in the name
   of a Being infinitely higher than themselves or their
   leaders to do so.
3. A *system of ethical laws binding upon an entire people*.
   Since Judaism has the above two things, systematically
   codified ethics and a higher source, Jews have a binding
   source of morality by which to judge and correct themselves and other Jews—they can say "you have violated
   such and such a law and God's will." In order to improve the ethical behavior of religious Jews we can
   appeal to Judaism. Should a humanist perpetrate evil,
   what can we say to him—"Human experience, reason,
   the editor of *The Humanist* suggest that you act dif-
   ferently?"
4. A *way to transmit a system of ethics*. For over three

thousand years Judaism has had its ethics transmitted from generation to generation through the study of Judaism and observance of its laws. What is the system by which ethical ideals are transmitted from the humanist parent to his or her child? Is not humanism at a distinct disadvantage because it lacks such a system?

CONCLUSION

Which is more likely to create ethical individuals, secular humanism or religious humanism, ethical humanism or ethical monotheism, humanist ideals or Jewish practices and ideals, well-intentioned individuals or a religiously motivated nation?

Question 5

WHAT IS THE JEWISH ROLE IN THE WORLD?

Israel's great achievement, so apparent that mention of it is almost trite, was mono-theism. It was an achievement that trans-formed subsequent history. . . . One may raise the question whether any other single contribution from whatever source since hu-man culture emerged from the stone ages has had the far-reaching effect upon history that Israel in this regard has exerted both through mediums of Christianity and Islam and di-rectly through the world of Jewish thinkers themselves.

 —H. AND H. A. FRANKFORT, JOHN A. WILSON, THORKILD JACOBSEN, WILLIAM IRWIN, *The Intellectual Adventure of Ancient Man*

The Hebrews have done more to civilize men than any other nation. . . . The doctrine of a supreme intelligent . . . sovereign of the universe . . . I believe to be the great essen-tial principle of all morality, and conse-quently of all civilization.

 —JOHN ADAMS, in a letter to F. A. VANDERKAMP, February 16, 1809

110

The Jews introduced God into the world, and called all people to live in brotherhood by accepting one moral standard based upon God. Each of these ideals, a universal God, a universal moral law, and universal brotherhood, was revealed for the first time 3,200 years ago, to some ex-slaves in the Sinai desert. Why this particular group of men and women, at that particular time, should have taken upon themselves and upon all their succeeding generations the mission to "perfect the world under the rule of God"* is a mystery which perhaps only the religious can hope to solve. Neither the God which the Jews introduced nor the task of perfecting the world which they assumed had any precedent in human history.†

"The idea," Professor of Comparative Literature George Steiner of Cambridge University has written, "of an invisible, unspeakable, unpronounceable god, *is perfectly unique. It happened once and once only,* so far as we know, and it is a maddening and crazy idea if you try to take it at all seriously." It ran completely against "the human instinct that rocks and trees and flowers and rivers and sky and stars are divine. . . ."‡

Whether one believes that Moses the "charismatic genius" or some other human phenomenon is responsible, or

---

* These words, over two thousand years old, are contained in the second paragraph of the *Aleinu* prayer, which is recited three times daily by observant Jews. See the discussion of this prayer in Joseph Hertz's *The Authorized Daily Prayer Book* (New York: Bloch Publishing Company, 1948), pp. 208–211.

† ". . . Israelite religion was an original creation. It was absolutely different from anything the pagan world ever knew; its monotheistic world view had no antecedents in paganism" (Professor Yehezkel Kaufmann, *The Religion of Israel*, Chicago: University of Chicago Press, 1960, p. 2).

‡ *Psychology Today*, February 1973; our emphasis.

that only divine revelation can explain what occurred at Sinai and the subsequent Jewish impact on humanity, the fact is that this people did take it upon itself to change the world. No matter how intense the suffering—and no people has had to endure the continuous slaughter and torture which the Jews have—this tiny people has persisted in what it never ceased to believe was its divinely appointed role to bring all mankind to the recognition of God and universal morality.

It is in this sense of a moral commitment to perfect themselves and the world that the Jews considered themselves "chosen." This consideration never meant advantages for the Jews, only increased responsibilities and hardships. If God did not choose this group of people to provide a moral model and improve the world, if in fact no divine-human encounter took place at Sinai, we can only conclude that this willingness of a nation to create and to take upon itself such a moral responsibility and burdensome way of life (and Jewish sources do refer to Judaism as an *ohl*, a burden) constitutes the most impressive national achievement in history.

Despite every conceivable obstacle, many of which no nation has ever survived (such as the loss of a homeland, dispersal throughout the world, and attempted genocide against it), the Jewish people has not only persevered, but precisely because of its chosen task, has succeeded in achieving what University of Chicago historian William H. McNeill calls the Jews' "world-transforming career."*

"It was Judaism," writes the Reverend Edward H. Flannery of the National Conference of Catholic Bishops, "that brought the concept of a God-given universal moral law into

---

* *The Rise of The West* (Chicago: University of Chicago Press, 1963), p. 166.

the world"; willingly or not "the Jew carries the burden of God in history [and] for this he has never been forgiven."* For the world to which the Jews introduced God and their new ideals of universal morality, justice, love, peace, and individual responsibility was not then, nor has it ever been, appreciative. Such ideals have generally been alien and threatening to the prevailing order. Judaism said that God and morality were higher than all gods, all leaders and all armies; that morality was universal, not relative to individuals, nations, or economics; that love was to be directed to one's neighbor and even to the stranger (*Leviticus* 19:34), not only to one's self or family. Judaism gave a vision that "nation shall not lift sword against nation" to a world in which war and warriors rather than peace and prophets were glorified; and Judaism said that every person is ultimately responsible not to the powerful, but to the Almighty. It is little wonder, then, why hatred of the Jew developed and ultimately became, as Father Flannery wrote, "the greatest hatred in human history."

Yet despite all opposition, Judaism's ideals continued to spread even as mighty empires crumbled. And twelve hundred years after Sinai, a group of Jews led by Paul of Tarsus, seeing the Roman Empire's pagan religions failing, felt the time ripe to bring the world to "the rule of God." With the dropping of Jewish laws and God rendered human, Paul believed, the world would more readily accept the "rule of God" and then be perfected. Thus began Christianity, the first major offshoot of Judaism.

Some six hundred years after Paul, in another pagan part of the world where Judaism's monotheistic ideals had begun

---

* *New York Times*, November 30, 1974.

to infiltrate, Muhammad revealed God to the Arabs, and soon the second major offshoot of Judaism, Islam, was born.*

The two new religions missionized aggressively and, as a consequence, the Jewish ideal made its way from central Asia through Europe to the New World. But its journey was a hazardous one which did not leave the ideal intact. The two daughter religions compromised on at least three basic tenets of Judaism. First, they emphasized faith (and in the case of Islam, predestination) over this-worldly action; second, they converted millions of people more by physical power than by moral suasion—and as a result they converted many more bodies than minds; and third, by converting so many people en masse, both religions (not to mention the original Judaic role) were diluted by pagan customs and beliefs.

Partly in reaction to the Christian overemphasis on the next world, a third, secular, offshoot of the Judaic ideal was founded by a grandson of two Orthodox rabbis, Karl Marx. This derivative, messianic socialism, or secular messianism, stressed only the perfection of this world. Marxism restructured the Judaic ideal to read: Perfect the world under the rule of man.

All the while, however, resentment against the Jew was building up among both those being subjugated to the Jewish offshoots and among followers of the offshoots themselves. Regarding the first, Professor Steiner writes, "the triple Jewish summons to perfection [Jewish ethical monotheism; Chris-

---

* "With Judaism [Muhammad's] acquaintance is intimate and many-sided. He learned his lessons well; and when a thorough-going comparison is made of the Koranic material, of all sorts, with the standard Hebrew-Jewish writings then current, we must say with emphasis that his authorities, whoever they were, were men versed in the Bible, in the oral law (Talmud) and the aggada" (Charles C. Torrey, *The Jewish Foundation of Islam*, rev. ed., New York: Ktav Publishing House, 1968, p. 61).

tianity and Islam; messianic socialism] built up [against the
Jews] murderous resentments in the social subconscious. It
made the Jew the 'bad conscience' of Western history."*

As for the followers of the Jewish offshoots themselves,
there was a constant resentment against the Jew for not join-
ing their particular summons to perfection; by refusing to
acknowledge the movements' authenticity and remaining
committed to the original Jewish role, the Jews constituted
the "bad conscience" of these Jewish derivatives as well. Thus,
the Church, from the New Testament through the modern
period, was never quite able to reconcile itself to the fact that
the very people to whom Jesus appealed were the ones who
found his appeal most wanting, and depicted the Jews as
"sons of the devil" (e.g., *John* 8:44) and treated them accordingly.†

---

* *Psychology Today*, February 1973.
† The medieval Christian depiction of the Jews as devils is documented
in Joshua Trachtenberg's *The Devil and the Jews* (New Haven: Yale University Press, 1941). Church legislation against the Jews was so all-encompassing that the Nazis utilized it as a model for their antisemitic legislation.
The Third Synod of Orleans in 538 legislated that Jews were not permitted
to show themselves in the streets during Passion Week; a Nazi decree of
December 3, 1938, authorized local authorities to bar Jews from the streets
on certain days. The Trulanic Synod ruled in 692 (a ruling reconfirmed many
times by Church leaders) that Christians were not permitted to be treated
by Jewish physicians; on July 25, 1938, the Nazis decreed the same. Starting
with the Twelfth Synod of Toledo in 681 the Church on at least fifteen
occasions burned the Talmud and other Jewish books, a practice later common in Nazi Germany. The Fourth Lateran Council in 1215, Canon 68,
decreed that Jews must mark their clothes with a badge; on September 1,
1941, the Nazis ruled the same. The Synod of Breslau in 1267 confined the
Jewish community to compulsory ghettos, and starting in the sixteenth century the Church helped enforce Jewish ghettoization throughout Europe; on
September 21, 1939, Heydrich issued the Nazi order confining the Jews to
ghettos. The Council of Basel in 1434, at Session XIX, ruled that Jews were
not permitted to obtain academic degrees; on April 25, 1933, the Nazis
passed the Law Against Overcrowding of German Schools and Universities.

And Muhammad, infuriated by the Jews' rejection of his claims to prophecy, changed the direction of Muslim prayers from Jerusalem to Mecca, and he expelled the Jewish community of Medina. Although historically less violent toward Jews than was the Church, Islam has always resented the Jews' rejection of Muhammad who, after all, based his Holy Koran on the Jews' Bible and religion;* and today the Islamic world has declared a mortal enemy every Jew who believes in Jewish nationhood.

So too, Marx could envision no emancipation for the proletariat until society was emancipated from Judaism, i.e., until the Jews ceased being Jews and assimilated into the working class. To this day, almost the only tenet which virtually every Marxist, Leninist, Trotskyite, and Maoist movement shares is the need for the disappearance of the Jews as a distinct entity. This is the main reason they consider every national liberation movement "progressive" except that of the Jewish people, Zionism, which they label "reactionary" (even when it is composed of Jewish socialists and workers).

Thus, the derivatives of Judaism always welcomed, indeed sought, the Jews' participation in each of their attempts to "perfect the world," though of course such participation had to be as members of the derivative movement, not as Jews. Jews who would convert to Christianity, Islam, or Marxism were assured of a life free from the sufferings which

---

Professor Raul Hilberg, who compiled this list, noted that the Germans could move so efficiently against the Jews because "German bureaucrats could dip into a vast reservoir of administrative experience, a reservoir which church and state had filled in fifteen hundred years of destructive activity" (*The Destruction of the European Jews*, New York: Quadrangle, 1961, pp. 4–6).

* See Abraham Katsh's *Judaism In Islam* (New York: Ktav Publishing House, 1954 and Herman Publishing, 1980, paperback) for an extensive analysis of the Jewish basis of the Koran.

they would experience by remaining Jews. Contrary to the myth that Jews cannot assimilate, the fact is that had the Jews converted to any of these majority religions they could have assimilated and indeed a significant percentage of Jews has always assimilated. Why, then, did the Jews not take the easy way out? Why have Jews felt committed to surviving at any personal price?

The answer lies in the mission which Jews have ceaselessly maintained they were chosen for by God: to serve, in the ancient words of the Prophet Isaiah, as "a light unto the nations," (49:6) and to perfect the world under the rule of God.

The Jewish people must fight for ethical monotheism against the two most powerful and popular world views: religious fanaticism, which emphasizes God and ignores ethics and reason, and secularism, which emphasizes reason and world improvement and ignores God. The first group includes those fanatics of all religions who care more about God than about people, who believe they alone possess the road to salvation, and who judge other people not by their deeds but by their beliefs. At the same time, Jews and all other ethical monotheists must fight against secularists who negate the fundamental elements of ethical monotheism—God and one moral standard. We are living during one of the greatest ideological confrontations in history—the battle between Moses and Marx.

Whether mankind accepts Moses's position that God is the highest being and that morality transcends man, or Marx's position that man is the highest being and that no morality transcends him, will decide the future of the human race. When God is declared dead, man dies as a value, and shortly thereafter he dies physically as well. Less than sixty-five years after Nietzsche announced that for Western man God was dead, the two ideologies based on God's death, Nazism and Communism, built humanity's first mass extermination camps. If, as Judaism posits, each person is created in the image of God, human life is sacred; but if, as Marxism and secularism posit, we are created in the image of matter, then we are only matter. And if we are but matter, the Nazi practice of making Jews into lampshades and bars of soap and the Communist practice of mass murdering for the sake of quicker industrialization must be understood as logical outgrowths of such a view.

That Marxism and other secular ideologies with their moral relativism are on the ascent after the horrors of Hitler and Stalin only serves to reconfirm the fact that people do not learn moral lessons from history and to confirm the fact that the Jewish role is confronting its greatest challenge in 3,200 years. But let no one prejudge the outcome of this battle on the basis of numbers or physical might alone, for Judaism has proven to be the most powerful idea in history.

For the last two thousand years Judaism has had to look inward. It is now time for Judaism to look out into the world and to offer itself and its ethical monotheist ideals as alternatives, and it is time for the world to look into Judaism.

We have learned from Christian experiences and Islam today that faith in God alone will not produce a moral society; from Marxism and Communism that faith in man will not produce a moral society; and from the secular intellectuals and humanists that faith in reason will not achieve moral results. There remains Judaism, the creator of the ideal of perfecting the world, the originator of universal ideals and equality—and a system which combines reliance upon God, man, and reason.

If all the fourteen million Jews lived by Judaism's values and means, the effect upon a world searching for meaning would be incalculable. If the hundreds of thousands of Jewish professors, writers, media people, doctors, and lawyers affirmed Judaism and did not suppress identification, as so many do, with the system which gave the world the ethics they claim to believe in; if every Jew lived the Jewish mission, fighting for ethical monotheism and against both religious fanaticism and secular radicalism, the impact upon all of society would be staggering. A moral revolution of unprecedented proportions would be in the making.

We also have, for the first time in nearly two thousand years, the opportunity to create our model state in Israel. Now nationally, as well as individually, the Jewish people have the capacity to show the world the moral power of the Jewish ideal.

In accordance with Judaism's 3,200-year-old directive (*Exodus* 19:6), the Jews must form an army of tender, caring, strong, moral people to combat the hordes of bored, aimless people and the religious and secular totalitarian and nihilistic ideologies to which they are prey. The offshoots of Judaism—Christianity, Islam, Marxism, humanism—now virtually dominate the world. Consciously or not the world has affirmed many of Judaism's goals, but it has altered its means. It is time—if there is time—to proceed with the world-transforming event which began 3,200 years ago at a mountain in Sinai—the Jewish revolution.

Question 6

Is There a Difference Between Anti-Zionism and Antisemitism?

> *Theoretically one can be tolerant of Roman Catholics and work day and night for the destruction of the papacy. Theoretically, one can be tolerant of Methodists and Baptists and forbid them . . . public dissemination of their literature. . . . In the concrete and specific, however, such distinctions are without a difference. No one can be an enemy of Zionism and be a friend of the Jewish people today.*
>
> —Franklin H. Littell, *The Crucifixion of the Jews*

> *When people criticize Zionists, they mean Jews.*
>
> —Martin Luther King

As long as one supports Israel's right to exist as a Jewish state, even when severely critical of certain Israeli policies, one is not an anti-Zionist. An anti-Zionist today is one who denies Israel's right to exist as a Jewish state.* The question is, then, can one support efforts to destroy the Jewish state and not be considered an enemy of the Jews, an antisemite?†

Anti-Zionists answer yes, arguing that whereas antisemites are motivated by opposition to all Jews, anti-Zionists are motivated by opposition only to the Jewish state and to the Jews as a people or a nation.‡

According to anti-Zionists, one who deliberately aims to harm or destroy the Jewish state (an anti-Zionist) cannot be

---

* We recognize that one can be theoretically anti-Zionist and still support Israel's existence as a Jewish state, since its destruction could not be morally defended. Such views are extremely rare and academic, and not discussed in this chapter. We are concerned with anti-Zionism as it is practiced and understood in almost every instance: opposition to Israel's existence as a Jewish state.

† We use "antisemite" and "enemy of the Jews" interchangeably since the term "antisemite" is only a polite substitute for anti-Jew. The term "anti-Semitism" was coined in 1879 by Wilhelm Marr, an antisemitic spokesman in Germany, to describe the then growing political movement against German Jews. The term is entirely a misnomer, however, since it has nothing to do with Semites. This also explains why we write antisemite as one word. We have adopted the approach of James Parkes, the distinguished Christian historian of antisemitism, to so write antisemitism, as not to convey the misunderstanding that there is a Semitic entity which antisemitism opposes.

‡ The Jews have always been both a nation and a religion (see footnote on page 42); but in order to legitimize their denial of the Jews' right to Israel, anti-Zionists deny that the Jews are a nation or a people, and assert that they are members only of a religion. A typical such denial of Jewish peoplehood is this statement from the charter of the Palestine Liberation Organization: "Judaism, in its character as a religion, is not a nationality with an independent existence. Likewise the Jews are not one people . . ." (Article 20 of the Palestine National Covenant).

121

likened to one who aims to deliberately harm the Jews (an antisemite). Or, to restate the anti-Zionists' argument, an avowed enemy of the Jews' homeland and of every Jew who identifies with it is not an enemy of the Jews.

For some anti-Zionists these differences between anti-Zionism and antisemitism may have some significance. For Jews, however, these differences are entirely academic. Though some anti-Zionists may sincerely believe that they are not motivated by hatred of Jews, *the consequences of anti-Zionism and antisemitism for the Jewish people are the same.*

Anti-Zionism differs from other expressions of antisemitism only in which aspect of Jewish identity it chooses to hate. Those medieval Christians who burned Jews alive also claimed (and perhaps sincerely) that they did not oppose all Jews, only those Jews who insisted on retaining their Jewish religious beliefs and practices. Anti-Zionists make the identical claim, differing only in which Jewish belief motivates them to oppose Jews. While supporting or actually engaging in the killing of Jews in Israel and attempts to destroy the Jewish state, anti-Zionists, like those medieval antisemites, deny despising all Jews; they only despise those Jews who insist upon retaining their Jewish national beliefs and homeland. And just as there were a few medieval Jews who gave up loyalty to the Jewish religion and were spared the hatred of Christian antisemites, so today there are a few Jews who do not identify with Jewish nationhood and are spared the hatred of anti-Zionists.

In fact, Adolph Hitler and the Nazis were the *only* antisemites in history to admit to hating all Jews, no matter what their religious or national beliefs. All other antisemites, like the anti-Zionists, have claimed to hate only those Jews who held certain Jewish beliefs. Unless the Nazis are to be considered the only antisemites in history, anti-Zionists are as antisemitic as every other type of antisemite. Only their motivation may differ. Like all other antisemites, anti-Zionists are at war with nearly every Jew (nearly every Jew has some sense of Jewish national identity and supports Israel's right to exist).

ANTI-ZIONISM AS ANTISEMITISM IN THEORY

Can someone deny that Italians are a nation, work to destroy Italy, and all the while claim that he is not an enemy of the Italian people because he does not hate all Italians? The question is obviously absurd. If you deny Italian nationhood and any Italian rights to their homeland, and seek to destroy Italy, no matter how sincerely you may claim to love some Italians, you are an enemy of the Italian people. The same holds true for those who deny Jewish nationhood and the Jews' right to their state, and who advocate the destruction of Israel. Such people are enemies of the Jewish people; and the term for their attitudes, even when espoused by people who sincerely like some Jews, is antisemitism.

An anti-Zionist would likely respond that the analogy between Italy and Israel is invalid, because "Italian" has meaning as a nationality, while "Jewish" has meaning only as a religion. And since Judaism is "only a religion" and Zionism is a national movement, one can oppose Zionism without being an enemy of the Jews or Judaism.

In addition to reasons already presented, this argument is false on four scores. First, it makes the extraordinary assumption that non-Jews can tell Jews what it means to be Jewish. As the prominent Jewish theologian Rabbi Emmanuel Rackman wrote: "I am a Jew and a Zionist. For me the two commitments are one. Furthermore, I hold this to be the position of historic Judaism. . . . I must firmly ask [non-Jews] to re-

124

spect my religious convictions as I see them and not as they see them."*

Throughout their long history, Jews have held that Jewish nationhood is, along with God and Torah, the basis of Judaism. In the words of an ancient Jewish text, "God, Torah and Israel are one." The Jews' self-definition as a nation with a homeland in Israel is not merely some new political belief of contemporary Jews, but the essence of Judaism since before the Bible itself was written.†

Second, the contention that anti-Zionists are not enemies of the Jews, despite their advocacy of policies which would lead to the mass murder of Jews, is, to put it as generously as possible, disingenuous. If anti-Zionism succeeded in its goal of destroying Israel, nearly all of Israel's three million Jews plus an untold number of non-Israeli Jews would die in their effort to maintain Israel. Both the Israelis and their Arab enemies know this. The Arabs, some Western-oriented propaganda notwithstanding, have repeatedly called for the destruction of the Jews in Israel during any future war with Israel. The Israelis for their part would fight to the last, both to keep Israel alive and because they have reason to believe that death is a preferable fate to capture by the Arabs. In the words of the Israeli Leftist writer Amos Kenan: "Shukairy [the head of the Palestine Liberation Organization before Yasir Arafat] used to say that the Jews should be driven into the sea. After the 1967 defeat, it became apparent that a slogan of this sort was not good public relations for the Arab cause. So today, only the Zionists are to be thrown into the sea. The only

---

* *American Zionist*, March 1971.
† The first of God's instructions to Abraham, the first Jew, is that he go and settle in the land now known as Israel (*Genesis* 12:1). Muslims, the leading anti-Zionists today, accept the Jewish Bible, but maintain that the Jews distort the Jewish Bible, since Abraham was really a Muslim.

trouble is that when the Arabs get through pushing all the Zionists into the sea, there won't be a Jew left in Israel. For not a single Jew in Israel will agree to less than political and national sovereignty."* Given, then, that if anti-Zionism realized its goal, another Jewish holocaust would take place, attempts to draw distinctions between anti-Zionism and antisemitism strike most Jews as demagogic.

Third, it was possible before the establishment of the state of Israel in 1948 to oppose the Zionist movement and not be an enemy of the Jews, just as prior to 1776 one could have opposed American statehood without being an enemy of Americans. Once the United States was established, however, anyone advocating its destruction would obviously be considered an enemy of Americans. So, too, once Israel was established, anyone advocating its destruction is considered an enemy of the Jews.

Fourth, anti-Zionists would be hard put to find any affirmatively identifying Jew who would not view them as mortal enemies. Studies and opinion polls have shown that 99 percent of American Jewry identifies with the right of Jews to the Jewish state.†

For religious Jews, as we have seen, Israel and Jewish nationhood are part of their religious creed. An anti-Zionist is therefore an enemy of religious Jews.‡ As for secular Jews, anti-

* "New Left Go Home," in Mordecai S. Chertoff, *The New Left and the Jews* (New York: Putnam, 1971), p. 311.

† See Norman Podhoretz, "Now, Instant Zionism," *New York Times Magazine*, February 3, 1974, p. 39.

‡ There is a fringe group of several hundred ultra-Orthodox Jews in Israel, known as the *neturei karata*, who are well-known enemies of Israel and of Zionism. At first, one might think that their positions are consistent with anti-Zionists. But this is not so. These Jews believe that the Jews are a nation (*Am Yisrael*) and that there should be a Jewish state. They insist,

Zionists oppose the *one* aspect of Judaism which they passionately affirm—Israel. The only Jews who could see anti-Zionism as anything other than an expression of antisemitism affirm neither Jewish nationhood nor the Jewish religion.

ANTI-ZIONISM AS ANTISEMITISM IN PRACTICE

Though they constantly deny being antisemites, in their writings and speeches anti-Zionists rarely draw distinctions between Zionists and Jews.* In order to hide their antisemitism, enemies of the Jews nearly always use the term "Zionist" when they mean Jew. This substitution often becomes ludicrous. On October 21, 1973, Yakov Malik, the Soviet Ambassador to the United Nations declared: "The Zionists have come forward with the theory of the Chosen People, an absurd ideology." This statement is a perfect example of antisemitism masquerading as anti-Zionism. An attack on Jewish chosenness is not an attack on Zionism: Chosenness plays no role in Zionism. It is a basic doctrine of Judaism. Malik's attack was consistent with Soviet, Arab, and Leftist opponents of the Jews who disguise their attacks on Jews and Judaism as attacks on Zionism. In the Museum of Religion and Atheism in Leningrad, an exhibit about Zionism and Israel designates the following

---

however, that this state should not come into existence until the Messiah personally establishes it, and since this was not the case with Israel (and furthermore, since the leaders of the state do not abide by the religious practices of the *neturei karta*), they do not recognize the current state of Israel. The *neturei karta* are as representative of Jews as the snake handling sects are of Christians.

* If one is to take anti-Zionists at their word, a handful of neo-Nazis are the only antisemites left in the world. Obviously what has occurred among the Jews' enemies is merely a shift of rhetoric. The Holocaust has rendered such terms as antisemite unusable, at least for the time being. Those who prior to Hitler would have called themselves, and been called by others, antisemites now utilize the term anti-Zionist. To the Jews, an antisemite by any other name smells the same.

as "anti-Soviet Zionist" material: Jewish prayer shawls, *tefillin* (phylacteries), and Passover haggadahs,* all *religious* items used by Jews for thousands of years.

A similar and characteristic use of anti-Zionism to disguise antisemitism was made in the *Black Panther,* the newspaper of the late radical black organization. Discussing the trials of Panther leader Huey Newton and of the "Chicago Eight," the article concluded: "It was a Zionist judge, Judge Freedman, who sentenced Huey P. Newton to fifteen years in jail. It was a Zionist judge, Judge Hoffman, who allowed the other Zionists to go free but has kept Bobby Seale in jail. . . . The other Zionists in the Conspiracy 8 trial were willing and did sacrifice Bobby Seale. . . . Once again we condemn Zionism as a racist doctrine."† The men denounced as Zionists include Jerry Rubin, Abbie Hoffman, and William Kuntsler, people who could best be described as non-Jewish Jews. The *Black Panther* attacked them because they are Jews (by birth), not because they are Zionists.‡

In the Arab world, "anti-Zionists" have adopted the calumnies of antisemitism and now spread them under the guise of anti-Zionism. The late president of Egypt and the leading political figure in the Arab world, Gamal Abdel Nasser, repeatedly cited the *Protocols of the Elders of Zion* (a forgery

---

* Cited in William Korey, "Updating the Protocols," *Midstream,* May 1970, p. 17.

† August 25, 1970.

‡ While the Left's antisemitism generally masquerades under the guise of anti-Zionism, the anti-Jewish writings of the Fascist Right usually acknowledge their animosity toward the Jews, seeing Zionism correctly as a manifestation of Judaism. Gerald L. K. Smith, the major disseminator of antisemitic writings in the United States over the past four decades, wrote in the *Gerald L. K. Smith Newsletter* of April 19, 1973: "The enemies of Christ are determined to capture the world—not through the United Nations, not through what people call a World Government, but through the manipulating, financial and military power of World Zionism."

128

purporting to be a document of the international Jewish conspiracy to take over the world, and a mainstay of Nazi propaganda) to document his charge that three hundred Zionists rule the world. King Faisal, leader of Saudi Arabia until his death in 1975, repeatedly publicized his accusation that Jews kill non-Jews and drink their blood. The Arab writer Saluk Dasuki published *America—A Zionist Colony*, a book which was widely distributed both in the Arab world and in the Soviet Union. In a rare display of frankness, Dasuki noted that "Jews, whether they have preserved their religion, or whether they have adopted other religions, are known in the United States under the collective name Zionists." Basing themselves on statistics in Dasuki's work, the Soviets published an article in the journal of the Young Communist League which asserted that in the United States, 70 percent of the lawyers, 69 percent of the physicists, 43 percent of the industrialists, and 80 percent of the owners of publishing houses were Zionists.*

Moral leaders of various faiths have repeatedly warned that anti-Zionism is antisemitism in practice. The late Dr. Martin Luther King said, upon hearing a black student at Harvard launch a tirade against Zionists: "When people criticize Zionists, they mean Jews. You're talking antisemitism."† In a similar vein, the President of the United Church of Christ, Dr. Robert Moss, commented on the anti-Zionist resolution passed by the United Nations General Assembly in 1975: "We should not be deceived by the use of the term Zionism. The sponsors of this resolution mean by it Jews and

---

* Cited in William Korey, "Updating the Protocols," *Midstream*, May 1976, p. 6.
† See Seymour Martin Lipset, "The Socialism of Fools—The Left, the Jews and Israel" in Mordecai Chertoff, *The New Left and the Jews*, p. 104.

Judaism as well as the state of Israel." The UN delegate from Costa Rica noted that the resolution was an invitation to genocide against the Jewish people.*

CONCLUSION
To deny that anti-Zionism is antisemitic on the grounds that some anti-Zionists do not hate all Jews is analogous to denying the antiblack racism of the Ku Klux Klan on the grounds that some KKK members do not hate all blacks.

Those who believe that they can deny Jewish nationhood and advocate the elimination of the Jewish state without being antisemitic, must do so out of a willful ignorance about Jews, Judaism, Jewish history, the Middle East, and the Arab and Muslim worlds. When anti-Zionists deny any Jewish rights to the land of Israel, do they do so unaware that in the past three thousand years the *only* independent states in the area known as Palestine or Israel have been Jewish, and that no independent Arab state ever existed in that location? When anti-Zionists work to destroy the Jewish state, do they do so unaware of how the Jews suffered during the two thousand years when their state was destroyed? Are Christian anti-Zionists unaware of the Crusades, the pogroms, and the other forms of relentless persecution of Jews under Christendom? Are Muslim anti-Zionists unaware of the second-class status, degradation, and violent attacks that accompanied the Jews in the Arab world up through the twentieth century? Are Leftist anti-Zionists unaware of the systematic destruction of Jewish life throughout the Communist world? Are anti-Zionists unaware that most of the six million Jews murdered in the Holocaust might have been saved had there been a Jewish state?

* See Sidney Liskofsky, "U.N. Resolution on Zionism," in *American Jewish Yearbook* 1977 (Philadelphia: Jewish Publication Society), p. 109.

In supporting the destruction of Israel, are anti-Zionists unaware that millions of Jews in Israel would be killed in such a war of destruction?

Whether the destruction of the Jewish national movement and the Jewish state, a holocaust of the three million Jews of Israel, and the subsequent abandonment of world Jewry to the good will of the world with no refuge of their own are carried out in the name of anti-Zionism or antisemitism is quite irrelevant to Jews. That today the people who want to do these things call themselves anti-Zionists instead of antisemites is an interesting historical fact. There may be some differences in which aspects of Jewish life anti-Zionists and antisemites hate, but these differences are of interest only to historians. Anti-Zionism and antisemitism both would cause Jews to be homeless, suffer, and die. And that is all Jews need to know about them.

Question 7

WHY ARE SO MANY YOUNG JEWS ALIENATED FROM JUDAISM AND THE JEWISH PEOPLE?

> *Many Jewish parents claim . . . that they gave their children everything that they did not have as children. The problem is, however, that the parents did not give what they did have as children—a basically Jewish environment.*

Next to the survival of Israel the issue that weighs heaviest upon Jews is the loss of Jewish identity among many young Jews. "How can we bring our youth back?" is probably the most oft-posed question in American Jewish life: study groups, symposia, and commissions are constantly being organized to answer this question. Yet too often we attempt to "bring them back" without understanding why young Jews have left, or as we (the authors) believe, why they were never really with us. We must first understand what has caused the alienation of many youth from the Jewish religion and community.

The essential problem underlying this rejection of Jewish identity can be summarized in a single sentence. For the great majority of young Jews who abandon Jewish identity, it is not Judaism but a caricature of Judaism that they are rejecting.

THE CARICATURE

Instead of portraying Judaism as the all-encompassing value system and way of life which it is, most parents and institutions today treat Judaism as if it were a pastime, an adjunct to the other, really important, things in one's life. Most Jewish parents repeatedly convey the impression that Judaism is of secondary importance. This can be illustrated in a variety of ways.

THE GREATER IMPORTANCE OF PROFESSIONS

Let us, for example, visit a typical Jewish home on the day when the promising young college junior or senior announces what profession he or she has chosen to pursue upon graduation. The proud Jewish parents are undoubtedly waiting to hear whether their child has decided on law, or medicine, or architecture, or one of the other professions which so many of our young Jews enter. But, alas, in this particular home, the young Jew reveals that he wishes to become a Jewish educator or enter the rabbinate or some other Jewish profession. After recuperating from their shock, the parents will probably protest loud and long against this decision which contradicts values they have been reinforcing throughout their careers as parents: viz., *what type of professional their child becomes is of far greater significance than what type of Jew he or she becomes.* And because Jewish parents have been far more interested in producing accomplished professionals than accomplished Jews, the Jewish community suffers from a surfeit of accomplished professionals who are alienated Jews. The irony is that later in life, many of these parents are saddened by the product which they so diligently molded. How often we hear parents speak of their "wonderful son" the lawyer, doctor, or professor only to add softly "who doesn't care about being Jewish." The pursuit of a profession is, however, only one of the areas in which young Jews are taught that Judaism is of secondary importance.

THE GREATER IMPORTANCE OF NON-JEWISH VALUES

Another reason young Jews become convinced that Judaism is of little consequence is that fearing that their children will become "too Jewish," many parents hold an attitude which may be called pseudo-universalism. This view posits that Jews must not smack of provincialism by raising their children with "too Jewish" an education, or in "too Jewish" a home, but must expose them to as many non-Jewish cultures as possible so that they may become "universal" and freely choose the lifestyle they want.

That such an approach to raising a Jewish child will produce an alienated Jew should be obvious. Unless deeply immersed in a minority culture, why would anyone choose to identify with that culture? There is no reason for any young Jew who is not raised in a profoundly Jewish environment to reject assimilation into the majority non-Jewish culture.

But this mode of raising a child will not only fail to produce a committed Jew, it will not produce a universalist either. The truly universal individual is first deeply rooted in a *particular* form of expression. The greatest literature, for example, is grounded in the individual, provincial, and national experience of the author. Dostoevsky knew and wrote about the Russian soul, not about everyone else's, yet individuals of every nationality read and learn from Dostoevsky's Russians.

To become a universal Jew one must first be an accomplished Jew. The attempt to be universal without roots in any particular culture does not make one universal, but merely alienated and confused. A Jew should understand and respect other religio-ethical systems,* but he must first know and live his own. If we studied everyone else's traditions and abandoned our own, we would not have increased tolerance, only fewer traditions.

As for "choosing," on what basis could a child, exposed

---

* This encouragement to study other systems does not represent a departure from Jewish tradition. Maimonides gratefully acknowledged his debt to Aristotle, while Bahya Ibn Pakudah (whose medieval *Hovot ha-Levovot*, "Duties of the Heart," is still studied in yeshivot throughout the world) not only learned from Sufi Muslim teachers but referred to them as *hasidim*, "pious men" (see Introduction to his book). Today, Rabbi Joseph Baer Soloveichik, perhaps the greatest living Talmudist, acknowledges the influence of Soren Kierkegaard, the nineteenth-century Protestant theologian, on his own thought.

to many differing systems of ethics, be expected to make an intelligent choice? By what standard can he measure differing religio-ethical concepts? When raised by parents who advocate universalism without particularism, a child has no standard by which to judge various lifestyles.

Many young Jews are raised in homes which communicate few clear-cut standards, and no distinctly Jewish standards. Therefore, many young Jews, lacking a strong value system, fall prey to any ideology that catches their imagination, or simply stand for nothing except self-expression.

In other crucial areas of their child's development, do parents present the child with a multiplicity of choices? Do they ask their children: "Do you want to brush your teeth, or would you prefer not to?" "Do you wish to attend school, or would you rather stay at home?" In any of these instances it would be absurd to offer choices to children, but in the words of Norman Lamm, ". . . a way of life that will determine whether existence has meaning, whether [the child] is rooted in history or not, whether morality is binding, whether hope and destiny are real or illusions—this any child may choose for himself."*

THE GREATER IMPORTANCE OF NON-JEWISH EDUCATION

Non-Jewish values are further reinforced by the manner in which we educate Jewish youth. By relegating Jewish education to a few hours per week for a few years (usually until bar mitzvah, precisely the age when a child can first begin to intellectually appreciate Judaism), we eloquently tell our children that we deem math, grammar, and social studies—all of which are studied more hours per week than Judaism—of

* *The Royal Reach* (New York: Ktav Publishing House, Inc., 1970), p. 310.

greater significance than Jewish history, philosophy, religion, and ethics. Furthermore, the unimportance of Judaism implied by the small quantity of Jewish study is confirmed by the generally low quality of Jewish education.

Most young Jews are given a Jewish education equivalent to between a third- and eighth-grade level, and then are expected to compare Judaism favorably with high-school-level and later university-level secular humanism, Marxism, or other philosophical systems.

Just as a poor education in chemistry will produce poor chemists or no chemists, so a poor Jewish education will produce poor Jews or no Jews; and the chances of alienation from Jewish identity increase even more in the proportion that secular education surpasses in time and quality Jewish education.*

ALIENATION FROM STRONGLY JEWISH HOMES

Less common but even sadder than the alienation of Jewish children who come from Jewishly inactive homes is the alienation of children raised in homes that are Jewishly active. Of these there are two major types: homes committed to Jewish causes but which are not religious, and homes which are also committed religiously.

---

* A personal note: We (the authors) did not acquire our fluency in Hebrew and familiarity with Jewish sources from attending Jewish classes for a few hours a week. Until the age of seventeen, we each attended a Jewish high school, the Yeshiva of Flatbush, where we studied Jewish sources for three to four hours a day (and we might add that this is no way stunted our social or professional development).

SECULAR HOMES

Many Jewish parents assume that their own deep attachments to the Jewish people should suffice to ensure that their children will retain a strong Jewish identity. Thus, one often hears parents lament something like this: "We can't understand how our child could intermarry (or follow a guru . . . or join up with radical—sometimes even anti-Israel—political groups . . . or care so little about being a Jew . . .); we gave so much to the UJA (or devoted so much time to Hadassah . . . or have such strong Jewish feelings . . .)."

Unfortunately, little comfort can be offered to these parents. It is extremely difficult to undo the mistakes which parents have been making for twenty years. But in order to help prevent repetition of such problems, it is important to try to understand where these parents went wrong.

At the outset, let us acknowledge one fact unequivocally. To ensure the Jewish identity of one's children, it is not enough to work diligently for a Jewish organization, contribute to Jewish causes, cry at Jewish tragedies, or possess a "Jewish heart." For while these aspects of Jewish life are noble and just as essential to Jewish survival as Jewish religious observance, they do not implant a strong Jewish identity in one's children.

One reason for this insufficiency is that children often do not perceive communal service as emanating from a particularly deep and sincere commitment to Jewish life, but rather as emanating from some professional, personal, social, or other need. Moreover, even when this work does in fact spring from a deep Jewish commitment, it may have little meaning for the child. For if the parents' entire Jewish identity is at the Federation office or at the Hadassah luncheon, what does the child experience Jewishly himself, at home? What distinctly Jewish

values have these parents taught their children? While becoming expert at *how* the Jewish people can survive, few of
these parents gave thought to the basic question their children
wanted answered: *Why* should the Jews survive?

At the root of this problem lies another. Many Jewish
parents claim, half in pride and half in sorrow, that they gave
their children everything that they did not have as children.
The problem is, however, that Jewish parents did not give
what many of them did have as children—a basically Jewish
environment.

The great majority of Jewish parents who work for or
contribute to Jewish causes out of a deep Jewish feeling
acquired that feeling by being raised in a more or less Jewish
environment. Had they given more thought to it, these parents would have realized the necessity of creating such an
environment for their own children.

As a result of the materially insecure existence of their
childhood, many Jewish parents concentrated on providing
only for the material needs of themselves and their children.
As we know now, however, affluence breeds at least as many
problems as it solves. When people do not have to worry
about their next meal or a roof over their heads, they have
time to worry about themselves and about such abstract questions as "What is the meaning of my life?" Our generation
can well appreciate the biblical observation that "not by bread
alone shall man live." We are the most affluent generation in
human history—and quite possibly the most troubled by being
unable to find meaning in life. When the needs for food and
companionship are fulfilled, the greatest human craving is for
meaning.

Thus, instead of reducing the need for a meaningful and
spiritual way of life, affluence and modern technology have

immeasurably increased it. The sad spectacle of youths from affluent homes who are utterly lost and fall prey to peddlers of pseudo-spirituality (e.g., gurus, Krishna devotees, Jews for Jesus) or misguided idealism (e.g., "revolutionary" and "underground" movements) confirms this fact.

Religious homes

Though less frequent, the alienation of Jewish children raised in religious homes is not uncommon. This alienation rarely includes a total abandonment of Jewish identity, though it can lead to that. Alienation from religious homes often stems from, or at least includes, a strong psychological component. Rejection of the religious beliefs and practices of one's parents is often but one part of a larger rejection of parental influence or one manifestation of a general rebellion against the home. Although important, however, such psychological considerations do not fall into our present area of discussion.

We must consider the rational and religious reasons for a child's rejection of his or her parents' religious observance. There are children from observant homes who come to view their parents' religious observance as little more than meaningless rituals based upon blind belief. While it is true that some children are content to continue religious practice out of habit, others who are blessed (or cursed) with intellectual curiosity will, as soon as they are exposed to the nonobservant world, begin to radically question the religion of their upbringing; and they may eventually conclude that their parents' religion consists of habits that are not any more worthy of perpetuation than their parents' other "personal" habits.

It is, therefore, essential for observant Jewish parents who live in contemporary society to fulfill at least two requirements in order to ensure that their children will continue to be ob-

servant. First, they must exemplify the ideals that Jewish law seeks to realize. Observant parents must be able to show that Jewish practice raises their level of idealism and ethics above the average person's; otherwise their children may regard their observance, and thus Judaism in general, as irrelevant, or even a barrier, to a moral or meaningful life.

Second, observant parents must be prepared to offer reasoned and meaningful answers to their children's questions. Certainly once a child reaches his or her teens, it is not enough to answer questions with "because that's what the Torah says." One of the uniquely impressive aspects of Judaism is that the religious Jew need not abandon reason. There are reasons to practice Judaism and there are answers to the questions which young Jews ask. It is the responsibility of parents to teach their children Judaism with reason as well as with passion.

We are living in a free society, in a huge marketplace of ideas. Young Jews are free to choose from among the many ideas and ways of life offered to them. We believe that Jews should deeply welcome this development, for Judaism is the most powerful idea in history (see Question 5) as well as a beautiful way of life. Until a great many more Jews, young and old, articulate this appreciation, however, the problem of alienation will continue to be a crippling one.

A NOTE TO PARENTS CONCERNING INTERMARRIAGE

A prominent rabbi told us recently that he had been called about three hundred times in the last decade by frantic parents imploring him to break up the impending intermarriage of their son or daughter. He agreed every time to meet the person, yet he succeeded exactly once in dissuading the person from marrying the non-Jew.

This negligible rate of success may prompt one to dismiss this rabbi as lacking powers of persuasion. Yet, this man, Shlomo Riskin, rabbi of Lincoln Square Synagogue in New York City, is one of the most dynamic and persuasive figures in Jewish religious life today. The number of young Jews he has attracted to Judaism is staggering. How then does one account for his inability to prevent prospective intermarriages?

The answer is sadly simple. Parents who approach a rabbi concerning the imminent intermarriage of their child are usually showing serious interest in their child's Judaism about twenty years too late. By this time, their son or daughter is already in love with a non-Jew, and the only obstacle to their child's complete happiness may be a guilty feeling that if he or she intermarries, "my parents would be distraught." But this will not ultimately affect their decision to intermarry, because they will refuse to sacrifice real feelings of love for vague feelings of guilt.

In most cases, the parents' approach to the rabbi, and their other efforts to prevent their child's intermarriage, constitute the first time that they have ever shown passionate interest in their child's Jewish identity. It appears quite odd to the child that all of a sudden Judaism, which until now was treated as a pastime, has become the parents' greatest passion. Had these parents shown a fraction of this Jewish commitment during the previous twenty years, their child would have taken Judaism more seriously and have become a less likely candidate for intermarriage.

Though numerous studies have confirmed the fact, one need not be a sociologist to recognize that intermarriage is rendered far more likely in homes which communicate the

142

caricatured Judaism described in the first part of this answer than in homes which live an active Judaism. Of course, one can point to the exceptional cases wherein children of actively Jewish homes have intermarried, but such pointing has no point. One can also point to instances wherein seat belts failed to save the lives of passengers in automobile accidents, but just as these instances do not negate the fact that seat belts save lives, so the exceptions do not negate the fact that actively Jewish homes save Jews.

Children from homes that constantly communicate by words and deeds that the Jewish people has a mission and that Judaism has distinctive values worthy of perpetuation are unlikely to intermarry simply because they are unlikely to find non-Jews (or, for that matter, many Jews) who share their values. If they should happen to find such a non-Jew, this is no problem, since the religion allows for conversion to Judaism.

The issue of intermarriage also reveals an interesting irony in Jewish life. When asked to characterize observant Jews, other Jews will often refer to them as "provincial" "closed-minded," and "too Jewish." Yet it is most instructive to note what arguments against intermarriage these two types of Jews can offer their children. The secular "universalist" is compelled to use family or ethnic arguments—true parochialism—whereas the religious "parochialist" can offer arguments which appeal to idealism rather than ethnicity ("Does he or she share your values?").*

The arguments against intermarriage of the less committed Jews are often ultimately rooted in the expressed or un-

* This is not to say that observant Jews always do utilize arguments based on values, and to the extent that they do not, they are guilty of the same provincialism as the ethnic Jews who oppose intermarriage.

expressed opinion that Jews are superior as a people (other-wise why not intermarry, since they obviously do not consider Judaism superior). Yet no seriously committed Jew should argue (or believe) that Jews are inherently superior. He should instead argue that Judaism is a superior system, and only in-sofar as a Jew inculcates this system is he or she more likely to be a moral person. Thus, whereas the Jew who lives Judaism can use logical arguments by appealing to a young person to perpetuate ties rooted in ideals, other Jews can only make an emotional appeal to perpetuate ties rooted in blood.

Numerous experiences have proven to us that it is never too late to begin to study and live Judaism, and thereby even-tually influence a child. If you are asking your child to make a life-changing decision, you must do the same. Otherwise your words will be as futile as they are (unintentionally) hypocritical.

Even if your son or daughter seems completely alienated from Judaism, or is actually planning to marry a non-Jew, or even if he or she has already intermarried, it may not be too late to influence him or her—and the non-Jewish spouse—to consider Judaism as a way of life. Of course, your ability to influence anyone depends upon your own commitment.

CONCLUSION

Mature people are open to new ideas, and Judaism may be characterized as a new idea for most Jews. Even many non-Jews who are married to Jews are receptive to studying Jewish philosophy, history, and theology and to begin to experiment with Judaism as a way of life, when it is presented with sophistication and warmth. We (the authors) have both met many men and women who after conversion to Judaism became leaders in their Jewish communities. We have also met a large number of people who, though born Jewish, came to take Judaism seriously only later in their lives, and who likewise developed into communal leaders.

Thus, it is never definitely too late. After seeing you infuse your life with deeper meaning, your children may also reassess their priorities and eventually realize the error of raising children without historical rootedness and without a religious-ethical way of life. We cannot, of course, promise any miracles. We can only promise you that if you show no commitment to changing your life, you will be offering little reason to your children to change theirs.

Question 8

WHY SHOULDN'T I INTERMARRY—DOESN'T JUDAISM BELIEVE IN UNIVERSAL BROTHERHOOD?

Many intermarried parents declare . . . that upon maturity their child will have the right to choose his own identity. This generally means that his identity will be with the majority group. . . . The majority of the children of intermarried Jews, then, will be Gentiles.
—MARSHALL SKLARE, *America's Jews*

These people [Jews who assimilate] . . . are lost from Judaism, that is all; lost down a road which has swallowed many more Jews than the Hitler terror ever did. Of course they survive as persons. But from the viewpoint of an army, it makes little difference whether a division is exterminated or disperses into the hills and shucks off its uniforms.
—HERMAN WOUK, *This Is My God*

This answer is the hardest for us to write. When we write of the centrality of the Jewish role in the world, the Jewish concept of God and man, or the sublime nature of the Shabbat, we appeal to reason. But when we write of our opposition to intermarriage, we must overcome your emotions as well as appeal to your intellect.

Questions 1 through 7 of this book are our answer to this question. If you have read them thoughtfully, we hope that they may have convinced you of the need to keep Judaism and the Jewish people alive. At the very least, however, it should now be apparent to you why we—and millions of other Jews—deeply care about your commitment to Judaism.

THE ISSUE: VALUES, NOT ETHNICITY

Our answer depends entirely on the values you share with us and your prospective mate. Do you care if the Jewish people and its distinctive values survive?

If you do, then sharing common concerns and values, it is relatively easy for us to communicate on the issue of intermarriage. We have only one question: Does the person you are considering marrying also hold these commitments and values? If the answer is yes, marry that person. Judaism welcomes converts.*

---

* Judaism so values sincere converts that it believes that the Messiah will be a descendant of a convert, Ruth. But the conversion of which we are speaking must be a sincere commitment to Judaism, not a *pro forma* gesture made to alleviate the bad feelings of anxious in-laws. Conversions that make no demands upon the convert to lead a Jewish life oppose all that Judaism

If your answer is no, however, then logic suggests the exclusion of this non-Jew, just as it would exclude a great many Jews, as a possible mate. In our personal experiences, we (the authors) have been involved in relationships with Jewish women which were eventually ended because to these women Judaism was likely to remain a peripheral concern.

If you are a committed Jew, we do not have to explain why you ought to marry someone who shares this commitment. Unless you subscribe to such romantic notions as "love conquers all" or that you can only love one person, it should be obvious to you that the more values and concerns which you share with your husband or wife, the greater the likelihood of a happy and successful marriage.

But what if you consider Judaism largely irrelevant to your life, or at least not something for which you are prepared to sacrifice a relationship? It is then far more difficult for us to communicate with you concerning intermarriage. Perhaps all we can do is address an appeal to you.

INTERMARRIAGE AND THE NONCOMMITTED JEW

We would begin by asking you not to reject a way of life which you do not know. And please do not fool yourself—you really do not know Judaism. The few hours of bar or bat mitzvah chanting, rote Hebrew, and spitball shooting which you probably experienced each week at Hebrew school simply

---

values. Such conversions render Judaism meaningless and render the Jewish people no more than an ethnic society. As should be clear from this book, we enthusiastically welcome converts to Judaism. But a sign-on-the-dotted-line conversion that demands nothing more of the convert is not a conversion to Judaism. It is merely a fraudulent solution to the problem of intermarriage.

cannot enable you to know or to judge Judaism. You may be able to judge the Judaism (or lack of it) of your youth, but the Judaism that has survived 3,500 years, the Judaism that bequeathed to the world God and universal morality, the Judaism that survived Pharaoh, Rome, the Crusades, Chmelnitzky (who murdered nearly one-third of the Jewish people in 1648), Hitler and Stalin, and the Judaism that today puts the Jewish people at the vortex of human affairs, is the authentic and powerful Judaism of which, sadly, you know very little.

We therefore appeal to your mind to begin to study authentic Judaism and Jewish history, and we appeal to your heart to begin experiencing Judaism as the beautiful way of life that it is. Once you have studied and developed intellectually and experientially as a Jew, you are, of course, free to reject Judaism. But we think it fair to say that rejection out of ignorance of the most significant moral ideas in history is intellectually unjustifiable; and the rejection of the Jewish people with its embattled 3,500 years of history, and its present battle for survival, is ultimately as self-denying as it is selfish.

In the eyes of the rest of the Jewish community, the intermarrying Jew is abandoning ship while committed Jews are fighting to keep it afloat. In addition to perpetuating the ideal of perfecting the world in a world which increasingly evokes cynicism rather than idealism, committed Jews feel a personal commitment to ensure that the Jewish people survive. Marrying people who share these commitments, creating a Jewish home with them, and raising Jewish children are the core of Jewish survival. In maintaining our ancient struggle on behalf of our ideals and our people, the Jews have answered Hillel's two questions: "If I am not for myself, who will be for me? But if I am only for myself, what am I?" Now you, too, must answer these questions.

THE POSSIBILITY THAT YOU MAY CHANGE

Consider the following: If you say that being Jewish has no meaning for you, are you certain that this is so? What were your reactions, for example, during the three weeks prior to the Six-Day War when it appeared that Israel might be annihilated? What were your reactions on and after Yom Kippur 1973, when once again the Jewish state was threatened with destruction? How did you feel when Israel freed the Jewish hostages at the Entebbe airport? Did you follow the news on those days with no greater interest or frequency than usual? Do you generally feel as personally uninvolved in Israel's struggles as your non-Jewish friends and co-workers most likely do? How did you react to the television production of *Holocaust*? If indeed your emotional reactions to these events was in no way exceptional, perhaps being Jewish really does mean little or nothing to you.

But, if the Nazi Holocaust, or the possibility of Jews again being slaughtered (in Israel, or elsewhere), or the disappearance of the Jewish people through assimilation affects you emotionally more than it does your non-Jewish friends, chances are that being Jewish means more, perhaps much more, to you than you think. And it is eminently possible that in the near future it will come to mean far more than at present. In fact, should such a change take place, you will be in good company. Many of the foremost Jewish leaders of the last hundred years were people who in their youth were completely disinterested in being Jewish, and who only later in their lives came to realize the centrality of Judaism to themselves and to the world.

Theodor Herzl, the founder of modern Zionism and the man ultimately most responsible for the creation of Israel, was an assimilated Jew until he discovered how profoundly Jewish he was during the Dreyfus case in 1894 when he heard French mobs shouting "Death to the Jews."

When Moses Hess, *the man who converted Friedrich Engels to socialism* and influenced the young Marx, was in his twenties, he considered Judaism irrelevant. Yet within two decades, this father of socialism broke with Marx and Engels over the amoral nature of their ideology, and Moses Hess devoted all his later years to working for Judaism and the Jewish people. His book *Rome and Jerusalem*, written in 1862, begins as follows:

> Here I stand once more, *after twenty years of estrangement,* in the midst of my people; I participate in its holy days of joy and mourning, its memories and hopes, its spiritual struggles in its own house and with the people among which it lives. . . . A thought which I had stifled forever within my heart is again vividly present with me; the thought of my nationality, inseparable from the inheritance of my ancestors, the Holy Land and the eternal city, *the birthplace of the belief in the divine unity of life and in the future brotherhood of all men.* This thought buried alive, had for years throbbed in my sealed heart, demanding outlet. But I lacked the energy necessary for the transition from a path as apparently remote from Judaism as mine was, to that new path which appeared before me in the hazy distance.*

Another such Jew was a Russian poet of such extraordinary talent that Maxim Gorki, the father of Soviet literature, predicted that he would become one of the great Russian

---

* *Rome and Jerusalem*, M. Waxman, transl. (New York: Bloch Publishing Company, 1918); emphases ours.

writers. Yet, with apparent suddenness, Vladimir Jabotinsky decided that it was more important to help fellow Jews establish their own homeland than to devote his life to poetry.

Had you asked any of these men when they were twenty years old if being Jewish was of any significance to them, let alone a reason not to intermarry, they would have probably ridiculed the question. Yet within a few years each of these men discovered that being a Jew was the most important thing in his life.

Since a similar change in your own philosophy of life and identification is a real possibility, consider how you would feel should you discover one day when Israel or Jews elsewhere were in great danger, that while you were deeply troubled, your spouse did not care nearly as much as you, or perhaps not at all. Or consider how you would feel if you wanted to contribute to a Jewish cause and your spouse objected. Or consider how self-conscious you might feel should you decide one day to start reading about Jewish history or Judaism. We are not asking you to imagine the impossible, for we have repeatedly come across sad cases (including marriages between two Jews) wherein one spouse begins to feel much more for Judaism and/or the Jewish people than does the other.

This development can become a major source of tension, for once you have incorporated ideals into your life they are not easily lost. Unless you are certain that being a Jew is never likely to be a factor of significance in your life, it is advisable that you discuss your present and potential Jewishness with your potential spouse.

You may also wish to take some time out to better know yourself as a Jew or to introduce both you and your potential spouse to Judaism and to Jewish life. Once both of you have studied Judaism and experienced Jewish life, you will be in a far better position to assess how important your Jewishness will likely be to you and to your marriage. You will be able to ascertain which one of three possibilities is likely to materialize: your being Jewish is unlikely to ever be important to either of you; under certain circumstances (such as when you have children, or at Christmas time, or with an eruption of antisemitism in our society) your being Jewish is likely to be important to you and therefore intermarriage is inadvisable; or Judaism has begun to interest your non-Jewish friend, and he or she may want to convert. Whatever your conclusion after studying and experiencing Jewish life, your consideration of the question will greatly reduce the likelihood of your Jewishness becoming a source of marital tension.

Marriage is difficult enough without the added problem of differing values, religions, and roots. Before you intermarry, a dispassionate consideration of this potential source of tension can only help.

THE EFFECT OF INTERMARRIAGE ON YOUR CHILDREN

As a final consideration, we would ask you to recognize the effects which your intermarriage will have on your children. First, and most obvious, you should be aware that your children are not likely to grow up as Jews. This is a fact of contemporary life as reported by the foremost sociologist of American Jewry, Marshall Sklare: "Many intermarried parents declare . . . that upon maturity their child will have the right to choose his own identity. This generally means that his identity will be with the majority group. Only if the child has formed a particularly strong identification with the parent who is Jewish will he be motivated to integrate into the minority community. *The majority of the children of intermarried Jews, then, will be Gentiles. . . ."* *

Admittedly, the likelihood of your children not growing up as Jews may not particularly disturb you. But there are two other negative effects of intermarriage upon children which should disturb you irrespective of your present feelings toward Judaism.

NO SOURCE FROM WHICH TO RECEIVE MORAL GUIDANCE

Since neither you nor your spouse strongly affirm your respective religions and yet neither of you wishes to convert to the other's religion, your children cannot be raised in a religious way of life. In order not to offend either spouse, neither Judaism nor Christianity will be practiced authentically; and it is wrong to assume that some innocuous hybrid of the two religions can be constructed so as to communicate the ethics of both. There are significant differences between Judaism and Christianity (see Question 4) and the attempt to amalgamate the two will not lead to an amalgamated religion, but to no religion at all. In the words of George Santayana, "to attempt to be religious without practicing a specific religion is as possible as attempting to speak without a specific language."

As for ethical instruction without religion, as we have noted on a number of occasions, telling one's children to be ethical does not suffice to render them ethical; an ethical system is needed, it must be based upon religious values, and in any event no comparable secular system of ethical instruction exists.

* *America's Jews* (New York: Random House, 1971), p. 202; emphasis ours.

154

If not from a religious system in the home, then where else will your children derive ethical values strong enough to withstand a lifetime of challenges? "What contemporary social institution can be counted on to give Western man a strong sense of moral direction? The university? The mass media? The corporation? The country club? The laboratory? The couch? Today only religious faith . . . can provide the basis for a social ethic worthy of the name. . . ."*†

EXISTENTIAL LONELINESS

There is yet another negative effect which intermarriages have on children. You will have effectively cut them off from identification with any community. Instead of affirming for yourself and passing onto your children what so many lost and lonely individuals in modern societies desperately seek, a sense of rootedness and kinship with others, you will have utterly cut yourself and your children off from belonging to anything beyond your immediate family. You are thereby bequeathing to your children the single greatest source of unhappiness in the modern world: alienation.

Consider this empirically based observation of C. G. Jung, one of the most important psychoanalysts of the twentieth century:

I should like to call attention to the following facts. During the past thirty years people from all civilized countries of the

---

* Eugene Borowitz, in Himmelfarb, ed., *The Condition of Jewish Belief* (New York: Macmillan, 1969), p. 32.

† Unless the home provides a source of firm moral education and guidance, a child will learn his or her values (or nonvalues) from the street and from television. As discussed in Question 6, a lack of moral education is common in nonintermarried homes as well. But at least if two Jewish parents realize the error of not rearing their children in a religious-ethical system, the only obstacle they will have to overcome is ignorance of Judaism. In an intermarried home the obstacles are only too obvious.

earth have consulted me. I have treated many hundreds of patients, the largest number being Protestants, the smaller number Jews, and [about] five or six believing Catholics. *Among all my patients in the second half of life—that is to say, over thirty-five—there has not been one whose problem in the last resort was not that of finding a religious outlook on life. It is safe to say that every one of them fell ill because he had lost that which the living religions of every age have given to their followers, and none of them has been really healed who did not regain his religious outlook.* *

When we consider the Jewish alternative to this self-imposed alienation, the tragedy of this cutting of Jewish roots is revealed with even greater clarity. Jewish life is communally based (so much so that we possess almost no prayers containing the pronoun *I*) and is structured so as to endow each Jew's life with historical and communal meaning. When the Jewish child is born, it is a major event not only for the immediate family but for the community. When the Jewish boy is circumcised at eight days of age, it is not an antiseptic surgical procedure, but a communal celebration of the entrance of another Jew into the covenant with God. When the Jewish girl reaches her twelfth birthday and the Jewish boy his thirteenth, they do not celebrate it alone or at a party, but with the community as it confirms them as responsible adult members. When two Jews marry, their wedding is sanctified "according to the laws of Moses and Israel," again a community event. Should Israel or Jews elsewhere become targets of hatred and bigotry, Jews will join one another to raise funds, mount political pressure, and do whatever else may be needed to aid fellow Jews—people whom they have never seen, whose

* Cited in *Modern Man in Search of a Soul*, C. G. Jung (London: Kegan, Paul, 1933), p. 244; emphasis ours.

156

country they have never visited, and whose native language they most probably cannot speak. When the committed Jew travels anywhere in the world—from Morocco to Siberia to Alexandria, Louisiana (among the many places where we, the authors, can personally testify to having been beautifully received by fellow Jews)—he or she is not alone but finds brothers and sisters who take him in, feed him, and show him love. Finally, when the Jew dies, the community takes part in this aspect of the life cycle as well. The community ensures a dignified burial, mourns for this Jew, visits and comforts the relatives who are sitting *shiva* (seven days of mourning), and lights annual candles of remembrance for him or her.

The human being is a social animal, and from the beginning of time and in all societies men and women have united to form communities. Whether or not a person finds meaning and happiness in life depends, in part, on having a sense of kinship with others. The community of Israel stands ready to share with all its members its joys and sorrows. They did it for your great-grandmother and great-grandfather in Poland (or Russia, Germany, Syria, etc.) and for your parents in America. They will not do it for your son and daughter, because you have removed them from the Jewish community.

DOESN'T JUDAISM BELIEVE IN UNIVERSAL BROTHERHOOD?

This question is analogous to asking if Einstein believed in relativity. Judaism is the source of the ideal of universal brotherhood. The Jewish Prophets are universally recognized as the earliest and most impassioned advocates of universal peace and brotherhood.

But how are we to achieve universal brotherhood? Is the assimilation of the minority of Jews into majority cultures the answer? Is abandoning Judaism the answer? What sort of universalism is it that demands that smaller groups give up their identities? That is totalitarianism, not brotherhood. The only way to achieve brotherhood is through all people sharing moral values, while retaining ethnic diversity.

It is precisely due to our commitment to universal brotherhood that we so fervently advocate Judaism which, for reasons set forth in this book, we believe offers the most viable method for the realization of this ideal. When we ask a Jew to reconsider his or her decision to intermarry, this request has nothing whatsoever to do with negative feelings toward non-Jews, or with automatically positive feelings toward those born as Jews. It is based solely on our commitment to the survival of Jewry and the Jewish way of perfecting the world.

Question 9

How Do I Start Practicing Judaism?

There is a well-known story about a rabbi who, upon coming to a new congregation, was taken aside by the president and in a friendly manner advised not to talk about certain topics from the pulpit: Hebrew schools—because the children had to take music and dancing lessons and needed the afternoons for play; the Sabbath—because in America one was compelled to work on the Sabbath to make a living, and making a living came first; the Dietary laws, Kashrut— because it was only an ancient health measure, out of place in modern times and, furthermore, [it was] too much trouble for the women to bother with two sets of dishes. The rabbi, surprised at the counsel he was receiving, asked anxiously: "If I cannot talk about Hebrew schools and I cannot talk about the Sabbath and I cannot talk about Kashrut, what can I talk about?" The president replied in mild astonishment: "Why that is no problem at all; just talk about Judaism!"
—Samuel Dresner, The Jewish Dietary Laws

158

THE "NOT YET" APPROACH

When Franz Rosenzweig, one of the leading Jewish thinkers of the twentieth century, was once asked if he put on *tefillin* (the phylacteries that Jewish men are supposed to place next to their head and heart each morning), he answered, "Not yet." At that point in his life, Rosenzweig did not feel spiritually ready or comfortable with the idea of putting on *tefillin* —but he did not believe his unreadiness should, or would, be permanent. By answering "not yet" rather than "no," Rosenzweig made known his intention to continue to grow spiritually. Though he was not yet ready, he foresaw the day when wearing *tefillin* would be a natural expression of his Jewish growth.

In order to elevate themselves to the task of perfecting the world, the Jewish people must begin to answer questions about their personal observance with Rosenzweig's "not yet." "Do you follow the Jewish command to give ten percent of your earnings to *tzedaka?*" "Not yet, but I am giving more of my income each year." "Do you observe the Shabbat in your household in full compliance with Judaism's command to make the Shabbat day holy?" "Not yet fully, but we have started to recite the *Kiddush* [blessing over the wine] and the *Birkat Hamazon* [grace after meals] at our Shabbat meals. We have also been able to liberate our family from reliance upon the television, and we will soon be starting a Shabbat discussion group with our friends." "Have you done all that you can for Soviet Jewry?" "Not yet, but the whole family recently participated in a Soviet Jewry demonstration, and we are beginning to correspond with a Russian Jewish family awaiting a visa." "Do you observe the laws of Kashrut?" "Not yet entirely, but we no longer eat pork or shellfish."

The profundity of the "not yet" answer is that it is applicable to the Jew who has tried to observe Judaism for many years as well as to the Jew who has just begun to incorporate Judaism into his or her life. "Do you follow the laws of *tzedaka?*" "Not yet fully. Though I give ten percent of my income to *tzedaka*, I do not give enough time to good causes." "Do you observe the Shabbat in your household according to Jewish law?" "Not yet fully. True, I and my family do not violate any of the Shabbat laws, but too often I sleep away most of the day. So I am starting a *chavruta* [learning with a friend] every week after synagogue to make sure that I keep up with my Jewish studies." "Have you done all that you should for Soviet Jewry?" "I have not yet done enough. True, for years I and my family have gone to demonstrations and written letters, but now we have become active in the Student Struggle for Soviet Jewry and the National Conference on Soviet Jewry." "Do you observe the laws of Kashrut?" "We do observe Kashrut, but not yet in all its moral ramifications. So we are lending support to groups which protest and fight inhumane forms of hunting. Also, since there is in our community a large university where very few of the Jewish students keep kosher, either because they do not know the reasons for keeping Kashrut or because it is too expensive, some friends and I have made it known to the Hillel rabbi and to local Jewish student groups that we have an open home where students are invited for a Shabbat or weekday meal."

If Jews, individually and communally, were to start answering "not yet," it would remind us that in the search for God and goodness all of us are "not yet" there and that we therefore need each other's help. To paraphrase Jakob Petuchowski, Professor of Jewish theology at Hebrew Union College, this approach to Judaism will generate unity among all Jews whose pattern of religious observance derives from a desire to hear God's commandments. The "not yet" approach has inspired one traditional rabbi to write: "When someone who eats in a non-kosher restaurant orders beefsteaks instead of porkchops because he keeps kosher, I can no longer laugh at him. His choice was occasioned by a sort of low-level, yet very genuine, concern not to eat of [non-kosher] beasts. . . . When he refuses butter on it and milk with his coffee because of 'seethe not the kid in its mother's milk,' I respect him still further. And if he orders a scalebearing fish instead of meat, I see him struggling honestly to do God's will."*

As you read this section on practicing Judaism, bear in mind that we are not setting down imperatives that you must follow, nor do we wish to imply that we have mastered everything we suggest. If asked whether we follow everything we have written here, we too would answer, "Not yet." What we have set down are the activities that we have found help stimulate a dynamic Jewish life. This answer is certainly not meant to outline all of Jewish law, even in the areas discussed. It is only meant to be a beginning, to answer the question "How do I start incorporating Judaism into my life?"

May you go from strength to strength.

---

* Zalman Schachter, in Himmelfarb, ed., *The Condition of Jewish Belief*, p. 211.

SHABBAT OBSERVANCE

I cannot feel that the important issue in nonobservance of the Shabbat is sin, but it certainly is a missed opportunity which can never be recovered. A Shabbat that I miss can never happen to me again. I have lost it.
—RICHARD ISRAEL, in *The Condition of Jewish Belief*

The best way to start observing the Shabbat is by reserving every Friday night for a large and lengthy meal. This may not be easily arranged in the beginning, particularly for families with children, but after one or two months you will not be able to imagine a Friday night without the Shabbat meal.

We would suggest the following guidelines:

1. *Prepare for the Friday night meal and Shabbat all week.* If you have children, ask your young ones to make a Jewish craft or learn a Jewish poem or song to present to the family. Older children might review a Jewish article or book, lead a discussion, or the like.

   Save the best tablecloth and silverware and have everyone wear clothing that manifests the fact that the Shabbat is special.

2. *Light the Shabbat candles.*

3. *Bless the children.* This blessing, which is recited after the Kabbalat Shabbat, the Friday night prayer service, is said by parents. The father or mother, or both, place their lips on the child's forehead and hold the child while reciting to a son "May God make you like

Ephraim and Menasheh," and to a daughter "May God make you like Sarah, Rebekah, Rachel, and Leah."

Herbert Wiener, an American Reform rabbi who witnessed an elderly North African Jew reciting such a blessing in Safed, Israel, was moved to write, "I could not help but think of successful suburban fathers who had made comfortable provisions for their children, yet would never receive the honor and respect that had fallen to the lot of the old North African Jew who could offer only blessings."*

American Jews who have incorporated this custom into their homes have reported some other unexpected dividends. We know one family in which the children now reciprocate the parents' blessings with their own.

In another household, neighbors witnessing the ritual asked what gift the parents were planning to purchase for their daughter. They assumed that the parents had promised the little girl a gift because her face lit up after her father whispered something to her.

4. *Recite the* Kiddush. The *Kiddush* over the wine is usually recited by the father. In a coed student community or any gathering outside the family, anyone may recite it initially. It is also important to encourage small children to recite the *Kiddush* so as to train them in Shabbat observance and give them a feeling of participation.

At the end of the *Kiddush*, all present respond

---

* 9½ *Mystics* (New York: Holt, Rinehart and Winston, 1969), p. 257.

"amen," the reciter drinks from the cup of wine, and then the cup is passed around for all to drink.

The *Kiddush* stresses two motifs: imitation of God and freedom. On the seventh day we rest in imitation of God who created for six days and rested on the seventh. And on the Shabbat we are free men and women who work for no one.

5. *Wash hands before eating the* challah (*the special soft bread baked for the Sabbath*). Many Jews erroneously believe that the Jewish ritual of washing one's hands before meals is practiced for hygienic reasons. Jewish law demands, however, that one's hands be hygienically clean *before* this ritual washing. We immerse our hands in water and recite a blessing in order to endow the meal we are about to have with spirituality. This is followed by the cutting of the *challah* accompanied by the *Hamotzi*, the blessing, "Blessed are You, Lord our God, King of the Universe, who brings forth bread from the earth."

6. *Sing throughout the meal to help convey the joy of Shabbat.* The singing consists of the traditional Shabbat *zmirot* or other Hebrew or English songs suitable for the Shabbat atmosphere. You can learn the words and tunes through any of numerous Hebrew records that have been released in the United States and Israel during the last few years.

After hearing everyone singing and seeing the candles lit and everyone dressed up, a visiting six-year-old girl from a nonobservant home exclaimed, "Hey, what's the party for?" "We have such a party *every* Friday night," we answered.

7. *Recite the* Birkat Hamazon (grace at the end of the

meal). The meal concludes with an expression of gratitude to God for providing life, health, and sufficient food to eat.

8. *Study and discuss texts and ideas at the table and afterward.* According to the Talmud, "The Shabbat and festivals were only given to Israel to provide them with an opportunity to study Torah." It is particularly crucial today, when the Jewish community is by and large Jewishly illiterate, that the Shabbat meal serve an educational function. No matter what the age of the children, the family should study the Torah with its commentaries and attempt to extract the ethical meaning of its stories and laws.

The following discussion of the tale of Sodom and Gomorrah is an example of the philosophical and moral profundity to be found in one Torah chapter:

Genesis 18 narrates the story of Sodom and Gomorrah, two ancient Near Eastern cities inhabited and controlled by evil men. The Bible, in recounting God's decision to destroy these cities, relates a unique debate that occurred between Abraham and the Creator. When God informed Abraham of His decision to destroy the cities, Abraham protested and made an appeal: "Shall not the judge of all the world act with justice?" (18:25). He entreated God to save the cities if fifty, or forty-five, or forty, or thirty, or twenty, or even only ten righteous people were to be found within them.

God acceded to each of Abraham's appeals. When it became apparent that with the exception of one family the entire populace was evil, God proceeded to destroy the cities.

This chapter is a good example of how the Bible confronts a universal theme—in this case, evil—and outlines its ideals in a manner that makes the study of the Bible meaningful for both children and adults. Adults and children learn from this story that there are universal moral standards which are binding even in places like Sodom and Gomorrah (read Nazi Germany, the Soviet Union, and other totalitarian states), where evil is called good, and that evil deserves to be, and ultimately is, punished.

These rather obvious points, however, barely scratch the surface of all that is suggested by the Sodom and Gomorrah story. For thousands of years, Jewish commentators and philosophers, and ordinary Jews at their Shabbat table, have discussed other implications of this narrative.

(a) What is the significance of Abraham's debating with God? Does Abraham's challenge to God have any implications for us today? When should we protest to God, "shall not the judge of all the world act with justice?"

(b) Is an action good because God says so, or does God say it is good because it is good? This chapter seems to reflect the latter view, for Abraham implies that God's decision to destroy Sodom is not just unless God can morally justify this decision.

(c) Though we had read this story dozens of times and were certain that we had understood it well, we recently studied this portion with friends, and learned how wrong we were. We had always assumed that Abraham was pleading for the lives of the good people of Sodom and Gomorrah. But, our friends noted, if Abraham's concern was for the good people alone, he would have requested of God that *they* be spared. But nowhere does he suggest this. He appealed that *all* the people of the cities be saved should at least ten good people be found within them. Why? And why stop at ten?

The Hebrew Bible is the most influential book in history. One reason is that it is challenging and accessible to people of every age.

9. *Try to raise the level of your talk to the level of Shabbat.* If you have followed the first eight suggestions, the atmosphere at your Shabbat table should be qualitatively superior to the atmosphere at your table during the rest of the week. But one thing can destroy this beautiful scene—gossip. Therefore, *try to speak about ideas and issues rather than personalities.* Should you succeed in doing this, it will not be long before your Tuesday night meals are uplifted too.

10. *Do not watch television on Shabbat.* Television renders us passive; Shabbat is a day that challenges us to rely on our own resources. Television teaches us to kill time, Shabbat teaches us to use and sanctify time. According to the Nielson studies, a television is on in American households more than six hours a day. By keeping it off one day each week you will, on that day, liberate more than one-third of the time the average American family is awake. The Shabbat is a natural day, no "artificial additives" are permitted. So, read, talk, walk, sing, hug, laugh, and

sleep, but don't sit silently in front of the television set.

THE SHABBAT EXPERIENCE

As we pointed out in Question 2, the purpose of the Shabbat is to create a day of peace on earth. When conscientiously observed, the Shabbat produces an almost heavenly sense of peace in the observer.

Peace between people. The Shabbat experience should be shared. If you have a Shabbat meal at home, invite others to share it, especially people who must be alone on Shabbat. Share your Shabbat with widows and widowers, divorced and single people, and students. If there is a family of Soviet Jews in your community, invite them; they may have never participated in a Shabbat.

But, of course, reserve some time on Shabbat to be alone with those you love. Let the family rejoice *together* on the Shabbat. It is much more difficult to do on Wednesday.

Peace between people and nature. Walk through nature on the Shabbat to observe and appreciate God's wonders, but do not exploit that which you see. Don't pick a beautiful flower even if it is to be a gift for someone you love. Confine your giving to a verbal description of what you have seen. Luxuriate in your garden, but do not dig, plant, fertilize, weed, cut, trim, or mow. When you reenter your house, do not look around for what needs repair. The Shabbat is not a day for household chores. And, since we are not to tamper with nature, do not light a fire (*Exodus* 35:2) to cook, or to smoke. *On the Shabbat, let nature rest just as you do; let nature be free of domination just as you are.*

Peace between people and God. Take time out for yourself on Shabbat, to think, study, and reflect. Be internally creative. As Rabbi Moses Tendler of Yeshiva University has written: "For six days we share with the beasts of the fields a common goal—material sustenance. Only on the Shabbat day when we proclaim God the creator and man as one created in His image do we assume truly human proportion. To rest by lying on a hammock, ruminating on a large meal, would be a further mimicry of the animal world. To rest by spending the day in intellectual disquietude, by mind-wracking study of God and man, by fatiguing examination of the children's studies that week, is a uniquely Jewish concept" (in Himmelfarb, ed., *The Condition of Jewish Belief*, p. 241).

THE SHABBAT POTENTIAL

When you adopt the Shabbat, it becomes a beloved experience which you want to share with friends. The Shabbat ideal has the potential to transform a strife-torn world into a harmonious, peaceful one, a world preoccupied with amassing material wealth into one concerned with attaining spiritual greatness.

Remember: the more ways in which you differentiate the Shabbat from the rest of the week, the more beautiful the Shabbat becomes.

INVOLVEMENT WITH ISRAEL

Only if there are many committed Jews living in Israel will we be able to fulfill the Jewish role in the world, the creation of a Jewish society to serve as a moral model. Therefore, among the best things you can do for yourself, your children, the Jewish people, Israel, and the world is to *make* Aliyah, *i.e., go and live in Israel.* Just as a Norwegian can lead the most authentically Norwegian life in Norway, a Jew can lead the most authentically Jewish life in Israel.

Should *Aliyah* prove to be impossible for you at this time, we urge you to take the following actions to solidify your ties with the Jewish state:

1. *Visit Israel as often as you can.* Travel around the country and meet its people. Come to feel at home in Israel. You are.

2. *Live for a year in Israel.* If you are a student, this is relatively easy to arrange. There are openings at every Israeli university (and at many high schools), at yeshivot (most of which are restricted to either men or women) and other schools of Jewish studies, and at kibbutzim (which are in constant need of people who are willing to work in exchange for room, board, and classes in Hebrew). If you are an undergraduate, you should seriously consider spending a year in Israel even if it means delaying your B.A. a year. The year will give your life the kind of meaning that no academic degree can offer.

    Spending a year in Israel should not be confined to students. Everyone, no matter what his or her work, should live a year or more in the one Jewish country in the world and the one which has the potential to create a society based on Judaism. You need Israel as much as it needs you.

3. *Learn Hebrew.* This is a most important way to ensure a meaningful visit and/or a comfortable adjustment to living in Israel. Many Israelis speak English, but Hebrew is their first language and it is rapidly becoming

the second language of Jews everywhere. Hebrew is the language of the Jewish people, its Bible, and its prayers. To know it is a major step on the road to a fulfilling Jewish life.

4. *Learn about the issues in the Middle East conflict.* There is always increased support for Israel's right to live in peace and security when people know the facts of the Arab-Israeli dispute. See to it, therefore, that your friends, Jewish and non-Jewish, know the facts and are able to counter anti-Israel propaganda with the truth. To start, we strongly recommend reading *Myths and Facts,* a concise presentation of factual responses to Arab and Leftist myths about Israel published bi-annually by *Near East Report* (444 No. Capitol St., N.W., Washington, D.C. 2001) and available at $2.95 a copy. It is must reading for anyone who wishes to learn about and present the case for Israel.

5. *Appeal to all the American people for support for Israel.* The increasingly massive doses of Arab, Leftist, and isolationist propaganda make it necessary to argue the case for Israel before all the American people, not only before elected officials. Knowledgeable supporters of Israel must speak before service clubs, church groups, schools, and the like, in every community, to explain why American support of Israel is politically and militarily in the American interest as well as morally necessary. Should you be a member of any such organization, arrange to have someone speak on behalf of Israel. Richard Reeves, a non-Jewish journalist, criticized American Jewry for confining its pro-Israel efforts to Washington and a few centers of Jewish population. The time has come for "American

Jews . . . to take the offensive and argue the merits of their case for Israel without apology or self-pity."* Unless we organize popular American support for Israel, the Arab, Leftist, and oil-lobby attitudes will be the only ones heard.

6. *Support political candidates who show concern for Israel and other moral issues.* This support should not only be in money, but in volunteer and other work. Support for candidates who want to assure Israel's security raises neither the issue of dual loyalty nor of single-issue politics. Any candidate who advocates withdrawing American support from the only democracy in the Middle East conflict is certainly not morally worthy of political office in the American democracy.

7. *Give money to the United Jewish Appeal, Israel Bonds, and other Israeli causes.* American Jews have responded generously in the past (though the sad fact is that more than half of the Jews in the United States have never given to Israel), but the continuing crisis situation in Israel necessitates our responding even more generously in the future. Until now, we have met few Jews who had to forego vacations or postpone purchases because of their contributions to Israel. But with the current recession in the United States it is possible that giving to Israel will require some people to sacrifice certain luxuries. This will be painful, but it must be done. *Tzedaka* is not charity; it is justice.

---

* *New York* magazine, December 23, 1974.

AID TO SOVIET JEWRY

One of the distinguishing characteristics of Jews is their help-ing other Jews in need. Thanks to the efforts of Jews in all free societies, most Jews living under Soviet totalitarianism have thus far been protected from government-inspired anti-semitic violence, and more than 200,000 have been allowed to leave the Soviet Union since 1970. This work must be con-tinued for the sake of the millions of Jews who remain in the Soviet Union.

There are several independent groups in the United States working on behalf of Soviet Jews which have been doing ex-traordinarily important work. The pioneer group is the New York–based Student Struggle for Soviet Jewry and its affiliate, the Center for Russian Jewry (both at 200 West 72nd Street, New York, NY 10023), headed by Jacob Birnbaum and Glenn Richter, two modern saints. Though its yearly budget is under $100,000, this group is indispensable. It organizes demonstrations whenever needed, coordinates the telephone calls to Russia that keep Soviet and American Jews informed, organizes Soviet Jewry activities throughout the United States, and serves as the most reliable source of information on the current situation of individual Soviet Jews.

Another extremely important group is the Union of Councils for Soviet Jews, which has chapters throughout the United States. (For the name and address of your local coun-cil, contact the Union at 24 Crescent Street, Suite 3A, Wal-tham, MA 02154.) The Union also operates on small sums of money while consistently, and successfully, developing pro-grams to popularize the cause of Soviet Jewry.

It is also important that you work within any national

Jewish organization of which you are a member to ensure their active participation within the National Conference on Soviet Jewry (10 East 40th Street, New York, NY 10017), which coordinates the activities of many national Jewish organizations for Soviet Jewry.

To become involved in Soviet Jewry work you should contact these organizations. Meanwhile, here are some suggested activities with which to begin:

1. *Political pressure.* Support political candidates who show concern for Soviet Jewry; and express your gratitude to leaders in the movement to guarantee free emigration from the Soviet Union. Write letters to your elected officials expressing your concern for Soviet Jewry. If you do not, who will? Also speak to non-Jewish friends about the issue and ask for their support in the struggle for free emigration from, and religious freedom in, the Soviet Union.

2. *Correspond with Soviet Jews.* Correspondence with Soviet Jews is an activity appropriate for both individuals and groups. You can obtain from the above-mentioned groups addresses of Soviet Jewish "refuseniks," people who have applied to leave but have not been allowed. It is impossible to exaggerate the importance of this simple activity. When I (J.T.) was in Novosibirsk, Central Siberia, in October 1973, a local Jew, Isaac Poltinnikov, showed me his proudest possession—one hundred letters he had received from five continents and from fifteen states in the United States. At that time, Dr. Poltinnikov had been without work for the three years since he and his family had applied for a visa, and he, his wife Irma, and their

daughter Victoria had been subjected to terrible harassment and pressure.* The correspondence assured him—and very importantly assured other Jews who knew of him and were considering applying to leave—that though inside the USSR he was despised, overseas there were people who loved him and who were doing all that they could for him.

Aside from boosting the morale of the Soviet Jew who receives correspondence from abroad, this mail also puts the Soviet government on notice that this "refusenik" is internationally known, and that any harassment of him will be publicized. Such publicity saves lives.

3. *Adopt a family.* There are a number of steps involved in adopting a Soviet Jewish family. First, contact one of the above-mentioned Soviet Jewry organizations for the name of a family in need of assistance. You will be informed of the type of letters you can write, the type of packages to send, whether it is wise to try and telephone the family, and the types of political pressure to exert on their behalf. Such work provides physical and psychological assistance to the people in need, and the relationship that is formed can continue

---

* The Poltinnikov story gives a vivid insight into the lives of Soviet Jews who wish to leave the Soviet Union. After nine years of petitioning to be allowed to go to Israel, the Poltinnikovs were given permission to leave in 1979. Irma and Victoria Poltinnikov believed that this was just a KGB trick and refused to go (on different occasions the KGB had arrested them, subjected them to long interrogation, and killed their dog). Finally Isaac left, telling them that he would write as soon as he arrived in Israel, and that they should then leave. Isaac wrote from Israel, but the Soviets refused to allow Irma and Victoria to join him. Irma soon thereafter died of malnutrition (she was afraid to leave the house), and Victoria subsequently committed suicide.

for a lifetime. Should these Soviet Jews succeed in emigrating to Israel or the United States you can easily stay in touch with them.

Because the adoption of a family involves much money and effort, it is an activity that is particularly appropriate for women's and men's groups, clubs, youth groups, and the like.

4. *Organize demonstrations.* A number of years ago, a Soviet official was overheard commenting at the United Nations, "Why should we change our policy toward the Russian Jews? We have promoted our policy for over fifty years, while they [American and international Jewry] have been demonstrating for just a few. And we will be around long after their demonstrations have stopped." The task of world Jewry is to convince the Soviets that our demonstrations will continue as long as there are Jews forcibly confined in a country they wish to leave. Whenever Soviet representatives gather, Jews must be there to remind them that we have not forgotten their victims. This applies to Soviet artists as well as Soviet politicians. Should the Bolshoi, for example, visit any country where Jews are free, they should be greeted with leaflets and other forms of protest. We have nothing against these artists, nor their art. But the Soviets do not see art as a value in itself; and when these performers return home, the Soviet government analyzes the political repercussions of their trip. If in every city the artists visit, people protest, the Soviets may become convinced—as indeed they have in the last few years—that it is politically worthwhile to allow Soviet Jews to leave, and to free the prisoners of conscience, men

such as Anatole Shcharansky, serving lengthy prison terms for nonexistent crimes. Thus, protests must continue even though more than 200,000 Jews have already left. For it is certain that if our activities on behalf of Soviet Jews stop, the Soviets will stop allowing emigration and their situation will deteriorate to what it was when the protest movement started in the mid-1960s.

It is important to realize that demonstrations are for the whole Jewish community, not just for kids. The two Jews sentenced to death in Leningrad in December 1970 would have been murdered if it were not for demonstrations and protests. Demonstrations and protests work. Without them, Sylva Zalmanson and her husband Edward Kuznetsov would be in prison camps, if not in their graves, rather than in Israel, and tens of thousands of Jews who emigrated would still be in the Soviet Union. Demonstrations serve a real political purpose.

5. *Help Soviet Jews who emigrate.* Our responsibilities to Soviet Jews do not end with their departure from the Soviet Union. For over sixty years these people have been cut off from Judaism. The Jewish community must help integrate them into Jewish life. We must provide scholarships for children to go to day schools, encourage Soviet Jewish participation in synagogue and communal life, and open our homes to them for Shabbatot, holidays, and throughout the year.

6. *Symbolic observances.* A Hasidic rebbe once remarked that just as a Torah scroll becomes invalid if only one letter is missing, so too the community of Israel be-

comes in a sense invalid when any Jew is missing. As long as these three million Soviet Jews are missing from the world Jewish community, we must raise this issue on all appropriate occasions, such as the Passover Seder of freedom. We must constantly remember that only thirty-five years after a third of the Jewish people was extinguished, another fifth is in danger of disappearing.

LASHON HA-RAH (GOSSIP WHEN TRUE, SLANDER WHEN FALSE)

The Haffetz Hayyim, a great Lithuanian Jewish scholar of the nineteenth and twentieth centuries, and a leader of Eastern European Jewry, would exact a promise from rabbis that they would be as careful to refrain from gossiping and slandering as they were not to eat pork.
—Dov Katz, *Tenuat Ha-Musar*

A Hassidic tale tells of a man who went through his community slandering the rabbi. One day, feeling remorseful, he begged the rabbi for forgiveness, and indicated that he was willing to undergo any penance to make amends. The rabbi told him to take several feather pillows, cut them open, and scatter the feathers to the winds. The man did so, and returned to the rabbi to notify him that he had fulfilled his request. The rabbi then told him, "Now go and gather all the feathers. Though you may be sincerely remorseful and truly desire to correct the evil which you have done, it is about as possible to repair the damage done by your words as it will be to recover the feathers."*

As the story illustrates, gossip causes irreparable damage. It can destroy lives. Yet despite its terrible effects, *lashon ha-rah* is an offense that almost everyone commits every day.

Leviticus 19:16 commands: "Do not go about as a tale-bearer among your people." The word in Hebrew for tale-bearer corresponds to the word for peddler, the implication being that just as a peddler goes from house to house buying from one and selling to another, so does the gossiper. There is a peddling mentality to the gossiper. When we tell someone something very intimate or very negative about a third party (something we might even have been told in confidence), we expect to be told something equally intimate about that individual or someone else. We peddle one intimacy off for another.

One hundred years ago, a major rabbinic scholar, the Haffetz Hayyim, wrote a *two-hundred-page volume* based on Jewish sources detailing the Jewish laws of permitted and forbidden talk about others. Concerning this work, Norman Lamm, President of Yeshiva University, wrote: "This is not a matter of piling up violations in order to show the author's legal virtuosity or to impress the pious reader. It is a bold act of stripping an accepted social convention in order to reveal the enormity of the evil it begets and its dreadful consequences."†

There is an addictive quality to gossip which makes it very difficult to stop. But the harm caused by gossip and

---

* Retold in Hayim Donin's *To Be a Jew* (New York: Basic Books, 1972), pp. 52–53.
† Norman Lamm, ed., *The Good Society* (New York: Viking, 1974), p. 59.

slander, such as the destruction of good names, reputations, livelihoods, friendships, and families, makes it imperative that one who wishes to become a better person, let alone a better Jew, must attempt to cease engaging in *lashon ha-rah*.

First, then, you must be convinced that gossip is awful. Once you decide to begin fighting it, the following suggestions may be of some help:

1. Speak as much as possible about issues rather than about details of people's lives.
2. Sometimes it *is* important to speak of a person's negative qualities—as, for example, in a letter of recommendation. Otherwise, don't do so. The general rule is: Do not transmit negative information about a person unless it is essential that someone have this information.
3. Since speaking about other people's lives is so tempting and difficult to stop entirely, confine gossip to one intimate friend (such as your spouse) and end it there.
4. Try to avoid spending time with people who gossip. Either choose the company of people with elevated taste, or, if you cannot avoid being with gossips, try to change the topic. If necessary, tell them why you are doing so. Don't be offensive, but if it is unavoidable, offend them. It is better to offend the perpetrators of the gossip than to conspire in destroying people whose private lives are being dissected. Besides, in all likelihood you too will soon become a victim of these gossips.

If you find that your friends rely on gossiping for the bulk of their conversation, you may want to qualitatively increase

—even at the price of numerically decreasing—your circle of friends. In choosing friends the most effective guideline is to choose people through whom we can become better persons.

The next time you find yourself talking about others, remember this insight of Israel Salanter, the great Jewish moralist and rabbinic teacher of the last century. Rabbi Salanter noted that we usually confuse our priorities. *Normally,* he said, *we worry about our own material well-being and our neighbors' souls; let us rather worry about our neighbors' material well-being and our own souls.*

BLESSINGS, PRAYERS, AND *TEFILLIN*

"Blessings were instituted by the Rabbis as a means for directing man into the presence of God at all times, thus providing for the continuous preservation of contact with the Creator."* Abraham Heschel has noted that when we drink a glass of water "we remind ourselves of the eternal mystery of creation, 'Blessed be Thou . . . by whose word all things come into being.' A trivial act and a reference to the supreme miracle. Wishing to eat bread or fruit, to enjoy a pleasant fragrance or a cup of wine: . . . on noticing trees when they blossom; on meeting a sage in Torah or in secular learning . . . we are taught to invoke His great name and our awareness of Him. . . . This is one of the goals of the Jewish way of living: to feel the hidden love and wisdom in all things."†

For the Jew who accustoms himself to making *berakhot*

---

* Pinchas Peli, "Blessings—The Gateway to Prayer," *Tradition,* Fall 1973, p. 65.
† *God in Search of Man* (New York: Farrar, Straus and Giroux, 1955), pp. 45–50.

(blessings), there is a continuous sense of the mystery and grandeur of existence, a constant affirmation that we do not own the world but merely serve as its custodians, and a constant awareness that others do not have such blessings. Blessings ensure that religion is an active force in the life of the individual at all times, not just on selected holy days.

The most convenient place to find the *berakhot* and prayers is in the Siddur (prayer book). The Siddur is a sort of mini encyclopedia of Jewish life. As Hayim Donin has written: "The Siddur is study as well as prayer. It is moral instruction and ethical guidance as well as pleas for personal needs. It emphasizes *man's duties as well as his rights.*"*

Begin meals with the *Hamotzi*—the blessing over bread; "Blessed are You, Lord our God, King of the Universe, who brings forth bread from the earth." Try to learn the *Birkat Hamazon* (the grace after meals) and accustom yourself to saying at least some of the other blessings. (There are blessings to be recited, for example, when putting on new clothes, meeting a great sage, Jewish or non-Jewish, and upon seeing the wonders of nature). Though it is permissible to say *berakhot* and the prayers in any language, it is a far more gratifying and meaningful experience to know the Siddur in the original Hebrew.

Develop the habit of starting the day with prayer. As we pointed out in Question 2, *l'hitpallel* (to pray) literally means to judge oneself; and what better way to start each morning than with a few minutes of self-judgment and introspection? An integral part of the morning prayer service (known in Hebrew as *Shakharit*) for the Jew is the donning of *tefillin* (the leather straps and the containers holding Torah excerpts

---

* *To Be a Jew* (New York: Basic Books, 1972), p. 180.

on parchment) opposite the heart and mind. One who puts on *tefillin* gives the day a spiritual dimension. The great sculptor Jacques Lipchitz, a nonobservant Jew, was advised late in his life by the Lubavitcher rebbe to start wearing *tefillin*. Lipchitz described the effect of this religious act as follows: "I *daven* [pray] every morning. It is of great help to me. First of all, it puts me together with all my people. I am with them. And I am near to the Lord, the Almighty, I speak with Him. I cannot make any prayers individual, but I speak to Him. He gives me strength for the day. . . . I could not live any more without it."*

TZEDAKA

> "Everything in God's creation has a pur-
> pose," a Hasidic rebbe once told his disciples.
> "In that case," asked a disciple, "what then
> is the purpose of heresy, of denying that God
> exists?" "Apikorsus (heresy) is indeed pur-
> poseful," the rebbe replied, "for when you
> confront another who is in need, you should
> imagine that there is no God to help, but
> that you alone can meet the man's needs."

Tzedaka, often inaccurately translated as charity, means justice with compassion. It is the feminine form of the masculine
tzedek, which means justice. It is therefore quite dissimilar
from its English equivalent, charity, a word that implies a
generous deed beyond the call of duty. When one does not
give charity he is considered, at worst, selfish. In Judaism,

---

* *Reconstructionist*, February 1974, p. 20.

however, *tzedaka* is an act of justice, it is very much the call of duty. A Jew who does not give *tzedaka* has committed an act of injustice.

The Torah legislated *tzedaka* over three thousand years ago. It legislated that every seventh year all the people would have equal access to the land; that the owner of the land could not take all the produce for himself, and that he was even forbidden to decide which poor people (such as relatives or friends) would receive it (*Leviticus* 25:1–7); that every third year one put aside a tenth of one's income for the poor, and that during the other two years, at harvest time, "When you reap the harvest of your field, you shall not reap your field to its very edge, nor shall you gather the stray ears of corn. Likewise, you shall not pick your vineyard bare, nor gather up the grapes that have fallen. You shall leave these for the poor and the stranger" (*Leviticus* 19:9–10).

What must be appreciated here is not merely the Bible's humaneness but the extent to which Judaism legislates goodness. It does not depend on our hearts to determine how much "charity" to give. The Jew is obligated by Jewish law to give one-tenth of his net income to charity. Those individuals who cannot afford to do so should give as near to ten percent as possible, and everyone is also obligated to give substantial amounts of time to good causes.

See the appendix for specific examples of Judaism's systematic ethics with regard to *tzedaka*.

THE JEWISH DAY SCHOOL

Jewish education is morally and Judaically indispensable. Only a thorough Jewish education can prepare young Jews to lead lives directed by Jewish moral values. We live in a completely open society which offers us every option from unrestrained self-indulgence to self-suppressing cults. Why should young people choose to live by Jewish values which they have never learned?

Judaism is not a "faith" wherein belief suffices, nor is it a matter of "feeling" Jewish, as important as that is. Judaism consists of its own peoplehood with the Jews' unique history, language, and holidays, and its own moral/religious world view and way of life. Young Jews must be taught all this, or they will grow up with an identity they can neither live nor even understand. *A Jew raised ignorant of Judaism knows he is different, but he does not know why.*

The most obvious reason for a strong Jewish education is that it helps guarantee that Jewish children will be Jewish adults. If young Jews are not taught why to be Jews, they will have no reason to remain Jews. This is precisely why hundreds of thousands of young Jews have quietly opted out of the Jewish people. When there is no reason to be different, there is every reason not to be different.

There is only one institution that can teach Jewish subjects as seriously as non-Jewish subjects, offer young Jews a joyful Jewish experience with peer reinforcement, communicate to them that their parents really consider being Jewish as important as anything else, and make knowing the history of the Jewish people as important as knowing about the Pilgrims. That institution is the Jewish day school.

Only at a Jewish school can a young Jew learn what it means to live as a Jew. Fifth-graders at most Jewish day schools speak better Hebrew and know more about Judaism than high school students in most synagogue confirmation classes. At a Jewish school, Moses is as important as Washington.

But most important, a child attending a Jewish school has the *sine qua non* to establishing a healthy Jewish identity: peer reinforcement. His or her friends are also experiencing Judaism. He is not the odd one out if he has Shabbat dinners instead of Friday night parties or basketball games; nor does the Jewish school student lament the absence of Christmas— he and his schoolmates celebrate a major holiday every week (Shabbat) as well as the many other Jewish holidays throughout the year.

The case for the Jewish school is obviously strong and need not be belabored. Yet, there are a number of frequently heard objections to such schools which must be addressed.

The most common objection is that a Jewish school handicaps those who attend it in their later dealings with non-Jews. As Jewish day school graduates ourselves, we know this contention to be untrue. For example, graduates of Jewish high schools are notably successful in college. Unless we are speaking of certain ultra-Orthodox yeshivas, the fear that a Jewish-school graduate will be unable to interact effectively with non-Jews is groundless. In fact, the opposite may be the case. Since a Jewish-school graduate is more likely to understand and live out his Jewish identity, he or she may be able to relate to non-Jews in a healthier, more honest manner than most American Jews now do. Unlike most American Jews, who feel Jewish but do not know how to live it, the Jewish-school graduate can relate to non-Jews as a knowledgeable, living Jew.

A second objection to Jewish schools is the related one of provincialism versus universalism: We should be educating our children to be universalists, exposed to all cultures, rather than isolating them in Jewish schools. This notion, discussed at length in Question 7, pages 133–35, betrays a misunderstanding of the universalist ideal. Raising a Jewish child to have knowledge of many cultures without an intimate knowledge of his own only helps to produce a person without roots, not a universalist. A Jew must certainly have universal concerns, but he must first know himself if he is ever to be able to contribute as a Jew to mankind.

Another objection of many parents is that a Jewish school education is too expensive. They are right (though nearly all such schools do offer scholarships). Jewish federations must aid Jewish schools and all our Jewish philanthropic commitments must be re-examined. If American Jewry is to survive, its first priority in fundraising must be the building of Jewish elementary schools and high schools and the hiring of its most gifted young people to serve as Jewish educators.

Nevertheless, parents must, until such aid arrives, weigh their priorities. In deciding what type of adult and Jew you wish your child to become, you must determine whether the monetary cost of a Jewish school education is lower or higher than the human and Jewish cost of no Jewish school for your child.

There is one final objection which is probably the strongest, though the least often admitted. Many parents fear that as a result of a Jewish school education, their children will be "too Jewish." If by "too Jewish" parents mean more Jewishly knowledgeable, hence more Jewishly active than themselves, their objection is not to Jewish schools but to increased Jewish knowledge and practice. In such cases, arguments against Jewish schools only disguise the real issue: Many parents simply do not consider Judaism and the Jewishness of their child to be all that important.

However, if objecting parents are open to reassessing their attitudes, there is, as we have pointed out, every reason to embrace a Jewish school. There are many different types of Jewish schools to choose from: Reform, Conservative, or Orthodox of all varieties; community; nondenominational. Moreover, it is probable that because of a Jewish school, non-active parents will begin to share Jewish texts and songs with their children and to make Shabbat dinner with them—such things that unite the family as nothing else can.

We must teach children goodness through Judaism, and while the home is the key to achieving this goal, parents need all the assistance available. As far as education is concerned, it is the Jewish school that can offer this help.

LEARNING ABOUT JUDAISM: RECOMMENDED READING

According to the *Ethics of the Fathers* (2:5), "an ignorant person cannot be righteous." This is not because an ignorant person necessarily lacks the desire to do good, but because doing good requires one to know what good is. In order to act Jewish, one must know what Judaism is and what it demands. The following is a reading and study guide which should enable you to start learning what it means to be a Jew. The books represent various religious and scholarly approaches to Judaism, and bibliographical information is appended.

JEWISH THOUGHT
We enthusiastically recommend the books and articles of Eliezer Berkovits. Berkovits, formerly professor of Jewish Philosophy at the Hebrew Theological College and now a writer in Jerusalem, is among the most challenging thinkers in Jewish life today. His writings are rational yet impassioned,

scholarly yet accessible. Particularly important are his *Faith After the Holocaust*; his profound reflections on Judaism and Jewish history in *God, Man, and History*; and his steady stream of writings on contemporary Jewish issues usually appearing in *Judaism* and *Tradition* magazines.

Louis Jacobs is a man who writes books that have deceptively simple titles, for his books reveal an incredible erudition in almost all areas of Judaica. To read through Jacobs's footnotes and bibliographies is an exhilarating experience. Jacobs has the ability to deal with themes that have been dealt with countless times before, as in his book *Jewish Values*, and through his vast erudition to give these topics freshness and excitement. His *Principles of the Jewish Faith*, an attempt to extract the enduring relevance of Maimonides's Thirteen Principles of the Jewish faith, is a masterful overview of Jewish scholarship over the last two hundred years, and his four volumes of anthologies of *Jewish Law, Jewish Thought Today, Jewish Biblical Exegesis* and *Jewish Ethics, Philosophy, and Mysticism* are all excellent for high school, university, and adult study.

American Jewry has much reason to be grateful to Milton Himmelfarb. His informed and critical assessments of contemporary Jewish life and thought which appear periodically in *Commentary* magazine are important contributions to American Jewish enlightenment. Himmelfarb has performed another great service, however. In 1966 he invited thirty-eight of the leading Conservative, Reform, and Orthodox scholars in America to concisely describe their views on such issues as observance of Jewish law, the notion of Jewish chosenness, Jews and the "death of God." The results of this effort are evident throughout our book, for we have often quoted from this anthology, *The Condition of Jewish Belief*.

Will Herberg's *Judaism and Modern Man* is a most profound exposition of the contemporary relevance of Judaism. Professor Herberg, who traveled from Marxism to Judaism, had a vast acquaintance with general philosophy and political thought, and every page is informed with his exciting scholarship and wisdom. The book is not easy reading, but it makes a uniquely powerful case.

Herman Wouk's *This Is My God* is a moving and profound account of why one man has made Judaism the focus of his life and thought. Wouk, one of the leading novelists in America today, observes Jewish laws and spends at least one hour every day in study of the Talmud.

In 1953, Hayim Greenberg, a leading Zionist thinker, journalist, and activist, died, and unfortunately with his death it appears that much of what he wrote was forgotten. Yet the contemporary reader who reads the *Hayim Greenberg Anthology* or the two volumes of Greenberg's *The Inner Eye* feels as if he has discovered a prophet. From his moral condemnation of Stalinism in the mid-1930s while many intellectuals stood in awe of the Soviet mass murderer, to his denunciation of the moral bankruptcy of the American Jewish leadership in 1943 for not doing anything substantial for European Jewry, to his 1951 criticism of the Zionists for practicing Zionism without Judaism, Hayim Greenberg wrote with the vision, ethical scope, love, and courage of a modern Isaiah.

Viktor Frankl's *Man's Search for Meaning* is perhaps the most important attempt to articulate a psychological world view compatible with a religious approach. While acknowledging the significance of Freud and the sexual drive and Adler and the drive for power, Frankl sees as determinative the human's search for meaning. His analysis is particularly poignant because the story of his life is intertwined with the development of his theories. Much of Frankl's "logotherapy" evolved during the years he spent in Nazi concentration camps, and both are related in this work.

JEWISH HISTORY

Many Jews express pride in Jewish history though they know almost nothing about it. We will confine our suggestions to a few popularly written but scholarly books on Jewish history. We hope that these books, with their more extensive bibliographies, will constitute only an introduction to extensive reading in Jewish history.

In *Great Ages and Ideas of the Jewish People*, Leo Schwarz gathered some of the greatest Jewish scholars of the twentieth century to write assessments of the period of Jewish history in which they specialized, such as the Biblical Age, the Talmudic period, the medieval Jewish world, and the modern period. In terms of interest and information this book is the finest one-volume history of the Jews with which we are familiar.

Louis Finkelstein's *The Jews* is another anthology of scholarly essays, and it is currently available in a three-volume paperback edition. As evidenced by the subtitles of the three volumes—"Their History," "Their Role in Civilization," "Their Religion and Culture"—the scope of Finkelstein's work is broader than Schwarz's; and many of the essays are masterpieces.

There are a number of good introductions to modern Jewish history, the period in which most contemporary Jews are interested. Howard Morley Sachar's *The Course of Modern Jewish History* conveys extensive information on the emancipation of the Jews and their entry into the modern world. The book, a one-volume encyclopedia of modern Jewish history, is unsurpassed on most aspects of modern Jewish history, though weak on developments within Judaism. For an overview of Jewish religious history and thought in the past two centuries we recommend Joseph Blau's *Modern Varieties of Judaism*. The book is a fine introduction to the Reform, Conservative and Neo-Orthodox movements, but, as it is based on six lectures Blau delivered at universities in the United States, it is not a truly comprehensive work. A study of what has perhaps been the most dynamic movement in modern Jewish life, Zionism, is provided in Arthur Hertzberg's *The Zionist Idea*. In addition to a brilliant one-hundred-page introduction by Hertzberg, the book contains the most important writings of the leading Zionist thinkers.

For an American Jew wishing to better understand his or her own roots, which for most of us are Eastern European, an excellent anthology describing what life was really like in Eastern Europe is *The Golden Tradition*, edited by Lucy Dawidowicz. Dawidowicz has selected writings of Jews from all walks of life. The poignant selections convey a sense of what it meant to be a Jew in eighteenth- to twentieth-century Poland and Russia. As for the development of Jewish life in America, we recommend Nathan Glazer's short history *American Judaism*, and Arthur Hertzberg's *Being Jewish in America*, a brilliant analysis of contemporary American Jewish life.

Some of the best writing about the history and makeup of the modern Jew is contained in novels. One such work is Milton Steinberg's *As a Driven Leaf*, a novel about Elisha ben-Abuyah, the one rabbi whom the Talmud records as having left Judaism. The novel explores the tensions and dilemmas of a Jew who rejects Judaism on intellectual grounds but ultimately finds that he is even more estranged, on moral grounds, from the non-Jewish world. Another novel which conveys at least as much truth as any nonfiction work on its subject is Elie Wiesel's *Night*, a shattering novel based on Wiesel's Holocaust experience. A third novel, Isaac Bashevis Singer's *The Slave*, illuminates the dark period of the Chmelnitzky pogroms of 1648 (in which a third of European Jewry was murdered). It is also a beautiful *musar* (religious-moral) book.

THE BIBLE

The source of Judaism is, of course, the Hebrew Bible, the most influential book in history. It has three sections—Torah (Teaching), Neviim (Prophets), and Ketuvim (Writings)—and together the sections are known as the *TaNaKh*. Because of the Torah's importance and centrality—it is, one might say, the constitution of the Jewish people—it is read through every year in synagogue in weekly portions.

To appreciate the Torah you must study it systematically, individually and/or in groups. For study purposes there are available in English several excellent books about, and translations of, the Torah. By far the most readable translation is the 1962 version by the Jewish Publication Society, but it does not contain any commentary or discussion on the text. Highly recommended, therefore, is the Hertz Torah, *The Pentateuch and Haftorahs*, which in addition to the 1917 Jewish Publication Society translation includes an accompanying commentary by the late Chief Rabbi of England, Joseph Hertz, which provides a summary of many of the traditional Jewish commentators plus an analysis of the text with Rabbi Hertz's own religious ethical insights. The Hertz Torah belongs in every home.

A superb guide which sets the first book of the Bible in its historical setting and incorporates contemporary biblical scholarship is *Understanding Genesis* by Professor Nahum Sarna of Brandeis University. Sarna utilizes modern scholarship and archaeology to deepen the significance of the biblical texts, and few scholarly books give the reader as deep an appreciation of the Torah's unique ethical and philosophical teachings.

For the rest of the Bible, (the *Nakh*), the most useful set to acquire is the *Soncino Books of the Bible*. They provide the Hebrew text, an English translation, and a fairly comprehensive commentary. To better understand the make-up, motivation, and general message of the Prophets, we also recommend Abraham J. Heschel's *The Prophets*.

A scholarly and readable analysis on the biblical period, the origins of Judaism, and a scholarly Jewish response to many of the biblical critics, is Yehezkel Kaufman's classic *The Religion of Israel* as translated and condensed by Moshe Greenberg. Professor Kaufman, considered by many to be the greatest Jewish Bible scholar of this century, makes a convincing case for the great antiquity and complete originality of the Jewish Bible and religion. This is an extremely important book, but for those who do not have the time or inclination to read it in its entirety there is a summary of some of Kaufman's work by Kaufman himself in Leo Schwarz's *Great Ages and Ideas of the Jewish People*, discussed previously on page 191.

THE TALMUD AND JEWISH LAW

The Talmud has been one of the most controversial books in history, and on at least fifteen occasions in the last thousand years opponents of Judaism have publicly burned this work.

Throughout their history, Jews made great personal sacrifices to preserve the Talmud. Rabbi Yechiel of Paris declared before Queen Blanche in 1240, "We are prepared to die for the Talmud. . . . Our bodies are in your power, but not our souls."

But the glorious and tragic history of the Talmud becomes far less glorious and even more tragic when we consider to what extent the great majority of contemporary Jews are ignorant of the contents of this work. Any program of Jewish study must include a basic overview of the Talmud.

Such an introduction to Talmudic literature is contained in Louis Jacobs's *Jewish Law*, which includes thirty-one selections from the Talmud, codes of Jewish law, and responsa literature, all accompanied by an excellent commentary by Jacobs. Representative samplings of the engrossing nonlegal Aggadic (legendary and ethical) portions of the Talmud are compiled in the recently republished A *Rabbinic Anthology*, by C. G. Montefiore and H. Loewe. A summary of Talmudic thought on many issues is contained in A. Cohen's *Everyman's Talmud*, while George Horowitz's *The Spirit of Jewish Law* is a detailed eight-hundred-page overview of Jewish law in many different areas.

The Mishnah, the earliest written compilation of the oral law, is available in two English translations. One, *The Mishnah* by Herbert Danby, is a one-volume translation of the text with no commentary. The other, *Mishnayoth* by Phillip Blackman, is six volumes and, in addition to the textual translation, includes notes that cite the biblical verses which are the basis for the Mishnaic law and explain the meaning and significance of all the terms used by the Mishnah.

In the centuries after the Mishnah was edited (around 200 C.E.) there arose a large body of literature, the Gemara, commenting on the Mishnah (you may have a clearer idea of the relationship of this material to the Mishnah if you compare the Mishnah to the American Constitution and the Gemara to the Supreme Court cases which ruled on the contemporary meaning and relevance of the Constitution). Eventually this body of literature was codified into two major works, the Jerusalem (or Palestine) Talmud and the Babylonian Talmud (the Talmud contains both Mishnah and Gemara). For a variety of reasons, the Babylonian Talmud emerged as the dominant work, so that in general, references to the Talmud are to the Babylonian Talmud.

Fortunately, a number of recently published works in English make it now possible for anyone to learn the Talmud. The most exciting of these works is currently being published in Israel: It is a translation of the Talmud called the *El-Am Talmud*, edited by A. Ehrman and others. Sections of three tractates of the *El-Am Talmud—Berakhot* (blessings), *Kiddushin* (marriage), and *Bava Metzia* (civil claims)—are currently available. Accompanying the translation is an extensive commentary that explains the Talmudic terms and places the Talmud in its historical setting. There has also been available for over forty years the scholarly translation by Soncino Press of the entire Babylonian Talmud.

JEWISH PRACTICES

For the reader who wants practical advice on the observance of Jewish law and the incorporation of Jewish values into his life, there are a number of fine books available, of which we will cite only a few. The first, *To Be a Jew* by Rabbi Hayim Halevy Donin, is a guide to Jewish observance in contemporary life. Though Donin is Orthodox, the book has been acclaimed by leading Conservative and Reform figures. In this work, Donin sets down in 310 pages Jewish laws in areas ranging from Kashrut and Shabbat observance to charity, slander, and employer-employee relationships.

A second book, *The Jewish Catalog*, by Richard Siegel and Sharon and Michael Strassfeld, has become a Jewish best-seller in the United States. The catalog is a uniquely lively and creative guide to Jewish living. In addition to describing how to build a Jewish library and how to bring a lively and creative spirit to your Shabbat table, it is probably the one book that also tells you how to make a *shofar* (the ram's horn blown on the New Year) or how to crochet a *kippah* (Jewish headcovering). All three volumes of *The Jewish Catalogue* are highly recommended.

Samuel Dresner's *The Jewish Dietary Laws* is a model of how an oft-discussed theme can be presented in a fresh and provocative manner. Dresner's discussion of Kashrut should be read by Jews who observe Kashrut, so as to ensure that they understand the reasons for their practice, and by those who do not observe these laws, so that they may come to appreciate the relevance and ethical importance of Kashrut. As Dresner writes, "other people engage in diets for their bodies. We have created a diet for the soul. If the first is understandable, why not the second?" At the end of Dresner's book is a short guide to keeping kosher by Seymour Siegel. Siegel presents the basic Halakhic guidelines of the Conservative movement. One wishing an Orthodox guide to Kashrut should acquire Donin's *To Be a Jew*.

All of these books should occupy a prominent place in the house of any family concerned with bringing authentic Jewish traditions and teachings into its household.

BIBLIOGRAPHY

JEWISH THOUGHT

Eliezer Berkovits, *God, Man, and History*. New York: Jonathan David, 1979.

———, *Faith After the Holocaust*. New York: Ktav Publishing House, Inc., 1973.

Hayim Donin, *To Be a Jew: A Guide to Jewish Observance in Contemporary Life*. New York: Basic Books, 1972.

Samuel Dresner, *The Jewish Dietary Laws*. New York: Burning Bush, 1959.

Viktor Frankl, *Man's Search For Meaning*. rev. ed. Boston: Beacon, 1963; paperback, New York: Simon and Schuster, 1970.

Hayim Greenberg, *The Inner Eye*. 2 vol. New York: Jewish Frontier Publishing Association, 1953, 1964.

———, *The Hayim Greenberg Anthology*. Marie Syrkin, ed. Detroit: Wayne State University Press, 1968; published simultaneously in paperback.

Will Herberg, *Judaism and Modern Man*. New York: Atheneum (paperback), 1979.

Milton Himmelfarb, ed. *The Condition of Jewish Belief*. New York: Macmillan, 1966; paperback, New York: Macmillan, 1969.

Louis Jacobs, *Jewish Values*. Hartford, Conn.: Hartmore House, Inc., 1960.

———, *Principles of the Jewish Faith*. New York: Basic Books, 1964.

———, *Jewish Ethics, Philosophy, and Mysticism*. New York: Behrman House, 1967.

———, *Jewish Law*. New York: Behrman House, 1968.

———, *Jewish Thought Today*. New York: Behrman House, 1970.

———, *Jewish Biblical Exegesis*. New York: Behrman House, 1973.

Herman Wouk, *This Is My God*. New York: Doubleday and Company, 1959; paperback, New York: Pocket Books, 1974.

JEWISH HISTORY

Joseph Blau, *Modern Varieties of Judaism*. New York and London: Columbia University Press, 1964; paperback, New York: Columbia University Press, 1966.

Lucy Dawidowicz, ed. *The Golden Tradition*. New York: Holt, Rinehart and Winston, 1967; paperback, Boston: Beacon, 1968.

Louis Finkelstein, ed. *The Jews: Their History, Culture and Religions*. 3 vol. New York: Schocken (paperback), 1970, 1971.

Nathan Glazer, *American Judaism*. Chicago: University of Chicago Press, 1957; paperback, Chicago: University of Chicago Press, 1972.

Arthur Hertzberg, *The Zionist Idea*. Garden City, N.Y.: Doubleday, 1959; paperback, New York: Atheneum, 1969.

———, *Being Jewish In America*. New York: Schocken, 1979.

Howard Morley Sachar, *The Course of Modern Jewish History*. Cleveland, Ohio: World, 1958; paperback, New York: Dell, 1977.

Leo Schwarz, ed. *Great Ages and Ideas of the Jewish People*. New York: Random House, 1965.

Novels:

Isaac Bashevis Singer, *The Slave*. New York: Fawcett (paperback), 1980.

Milton Steinberg, *As a Driven Leaf*. New York: Behrman House, 1939; paperback, New York: Behrman House, 1975.

Elie Wiesel, *Night*. New York: Hill and Wang, 1960; paperback, New York: Avon, 1969.

THE BIBLE

Editions of the Bible:

The Holy Scriptures According to the Masoretic Text. Philadelphia: Jewish Publication Society, 1917.

The Torah: The Five Books of Moses. Philadelphia: Jewish Publication Society, 1962.

The Soncino Books of the Bible, edited by A. Cohen. London: Soncino Press, 1946.

Joseph Hertz, *The Pentateuch and Haftorahs.* London: Soncino Press, 1972.

Guides:

Abraham Joshua Heschel, *The Prophets.* Philadelphia: Jewish Publication Society, 1962.

Yehezkel Kaufman, *The Religion of Israel: From Its Beginnings to the Babylonian Exile.* Moshe Greenberg, transl. and cond. Chicago: University of Chicago Press, 1960; paperback, New York: Schocken, 1972.

Nahum Sarna, *Understanding Genesis.* New York: McGraw-Hill, 1966; paperback, New York: Schocken, 1970.

THE TALMUD AND JEWISH LAW

Phillip Blackman, *Mishnayoth.* 6 vols. New York: Judaica Press, 1964.

A. Cohen, *Everyman's Talmud.* New York: Dutton, 1949; paperback, New York: Schocken, 1975.

Herbert Danby, *The Mishnah.* Oxford: Oxford University Press, 1933.

A. Ehrman, *et al.,* ed., *The El-Am Talmud.* Jerusalem and Tel Aviv: El-Am-Hoza'a Leor Israel. In progress.

George Horowitz, *The Spirit of Jewish Law.* New York: Central Book Company, 1953.

Louis Jacobs, *Jewish Law.* New York: Behrman House, 1968.

C. G. Montefiore and H. Loewe, *A Rabbinic Anthology.* Philadelphia: Jewish Publication Society, 1960; paperback, New York: Schocken, 1970.

The Talmud. London: Soncino Press, 1935.

JEWISH PRACTICES

Hayim Halevy Donin, *To Be a Jew.* New York: Basic Books, 1972.

Samuel Dresner, *The Jewish Dietary Laws,* New York: Burning Bush, 1959.

Richard Siegel, Sharon and Michael Strassfeld, *The Jewish Catalog.* Philadelphia: Jewish Publication Society, 1973.

FINAL CONSIDERATIONS

In presenting the case for leading a Jewish life, we have described many of Judaism's basic ideas and ideals. In order to render them as easily recalled and as adaptable as possible, we offer this very concise summary along with some final considerations.

Chazak chazak v'titchazek. May you go from strength to strength.

Question 1 (*God*): If there is no God, there is no ultimate meaning to life, and there is no good and evil (only personal opinions about good and evil). This is why it is incumbent upon everyone, and especially the Jew, whose people brought God to the human consciousness, to live *as if* God exists and to advocate ethical monotheism, even when in doubt about God's existence.

Question 2 (*Jewish Law*): Since people are not basically good, goodness must be both defined and legislated. Hence, Judaism's preoccupation with law. The purpose of Jewish law is to produce good, and ultimately holy, people. A serious Jew takes Jewish law seriously. It is, along with ethical monotheism, the Jewish people's greatest achievement, and its observance is the only insurance of Jewish survival.

Question 3 (*Unethical Religious Jews and Ethical Irreligious People*): As an observant Jew, you must ensure that Jews who make a mockery of God and the Jewish community by observing some of Judaism's laws while violating its ethical laws are made aware of your displeasure at their conduct and at the very least are denied positions of leadership in the Jewish community. The Torah commands us: "You shall reprove your fellow Jew [when you see him performing a wrong]" (*Leviticus* 19:16). If you belong to a synagogue where the rabbi conducts classes in Jewish texts, urge him to teach or review the laws dealing with business ethics and ethical behavior.

As for ethical irreligious people, seek them out and explain how Judaism combines their ethical goals with a uniquely effective means to perpetuate ethics. Explain to them the Jews' moral role in history. The more people living this role, the greater its chances for success.

Question 4 (Judaism Compared to Christianity, Marxism, and Ethical Humanism): Christians, Marxists, and secularists offer their ideologies to better the world. Jews, to their own and the world's loss, do not. On the contrary, Jews have attempted to improve the world through Marxism, socialism, liberalism, and virtually every other ideology—but not through Judaism. It is time for Jews to utilize Judaism, their own moral ideology and the root of the others, to improve the world.

Question 5 (Jewish Role): While Jews must live Judaism, non-Jews need not. The Jews' mission is not to bring the world to Judaism, but to ethical monotheism. Only when humanity recognizes universal morality, based on the universal God, can universal peace and love ever be realized. The attempt to destroy belief in God, the source of good and evil, as made by the Nazis and Communists, has led and must continue to lead to Auschwitzes, Gulags, and Cambodias.

To the secular world, the Jewish people must emphasize that ethics without God cannot survive and that reason without God leads to evil. And to the religious world, the Jewish people must emphasize that God without ethics is idol worship and that God without reason leads to evil.

Question 6 (Anti-Zionism): That anyone who attempts to deny a nation its legitimacy and seeks to destroy its homeland and kill its inhabitants could deny being an enemy of that people, constitutes a classic example of the Big Lie. Anti-Zionists deny the existence of the Jews as a people, telling Jews that they are only members of a religion, and plot to eradicate Israel and its inhabitants. Yet, they insist they are not anti-Jewish.

Big Lies can be fought only by Big Truths. Consequently, anti-Zionists must repeatedly be exposed for what they are: as dangerous to Jewish survival as any antisemite in history.

Question 7 (Alienated Young Jews): Ask today's Jewish teenagers the following questions:

1. (If you own a dog): If your dog and a stranger were drowning which would you save first? Why?
2. The Nazis thought they were right in murdering six million Jews; you think that the Nazis were wrong. Is there a right and a wrong, or is it all a matter of personal opinion?
3. In 1959, the Israelis violated Argentinian sovereignty when they kidnapped Adolph Eichmann to Israel. Were the Israelis wrong?
4. If Judaism's purpose is to make good people, why not marry a good non-Jew?
5. Would you shoplift if you were certain you could get away with it? How many of your friends do you think would shoplift (or have already done so) under those circumstances? Are those who would (or did) wrong? If yes, would you tell them?

You may find some of their answers troubling. If so, remember that raising good people and good Jews is difficult and it necessitates an actively Jewish home and a serious Jewish education.

Question 8 (Intermarriage): Unless being a Jew is irrelevant to your life, marriage to someone who does not wish to become a Jew can easily develop into a source of marital tensions or force you to suppress your own Jewishness.

As for your children, they will grow up in no authentic religious tradition, and quite confused as to their identity. This is not fair to them.

The Jewish people with its mission is an endangered species; we need you and your children.

Appendix

TZEDAKA: AN EXAMPLE OF JUDAISM'S SYSTEMATIC ETHICS

LAWS OF TZEDAKA*

1. It is an affirmative command to give *tzedaka* to the poor of Israel, as it is said, "You shall surely open your hand . . ." (*Deuteronomy* 15:8), and it is said, ". . . that your brother may live with you" (*Leviticus* 25:36). Anyone who sees a poor man begging alms and turns away his glance from him and does not give him *tzedaka* transgresses a negative command, as it is said, "You shall not harden your heart nor shut your hand from your needy brother (*Deuteronomy* 15:7). *Tzedaka* is a mark of our descent from our father Abraham of whom it was said, "For I have known him, that he may command his children . . ." (*Genesis* 18:9), i.e. to do charity. . . .

    . . . A man should also take to heart that life is like a revolving wheel, and in the end he or his son or his son's son may be reduced to taking *tzedaka*. He should not think, therefore, "How shall I diminish my property in order to give to the poor." Instead, he should realize that his property is not his own but only deposited with him in trust to do with as the Depositor (God) wishes. . . .

---

* Taken from the *Abridged Shulkhan Arukh* of Rabbi Solomon Ganzfried, translated by George Horowitz in *The Spirit of Jewish Law* (New York: Central Publishing Company, 1953), pp. 142–46, and reprinted with permission of the author.

205

206

2. Every person is obliged to give *tzedaka* according to his means, even a poor man who is supported by *tzedaka;* since he is permitted to take charity, even if he has a small sum of his own provided it is too little to produce an income sufficient to live on. In any event, since he has wherewith to sustain himself, he is obliged to give *tzedaka* out of what he receives. Even if he can give only a small thing he should not hold back, for his little is considered the same as much from a rich man. . . . Anyone, however, who has only enough for his bare subsistence is not obliged to give *tzedaka,* for one's own support comes before anyone else's.

3. How much does one give to a poor man? Sufficient to his need, but only to one who receives charity privately in secret. To him the people of the city should give all that he lacks in accordance with the standard he was accustomed to before he became impoverished. But to a poor man who goes begging from door to door one may give a small gift according to his dignity. In every city such persons should be given at least sufficient food for two meals per day and a place to sleep. One should also feed and clothe the poor of idolators because of the ways of peace.

4. How much should one give to *tzedaka?* The first year a tenth of one's capital, and thereafter a tenth of one's gains each year. That is the middle way. It is most meritorious to give a fifth of capital the first year, and a fifth of gains thereafter. A person should not squander his substance, however, by giving away more than a fifth lest he himself become a public charge. This limit is during one's lifetime, but at his death, a person may give up to a third of his wealth to *tzedaka.*

5. The tenth may not be used for general worthy purposes like candles for the synagogue or similiar things, it must be given only to the poor. However, if the *mitzvah* which one has occasion to perform is to officiate at a *berit* (circumcision) or to

conduct a needy bride and groom to the *huppah* (wedding canopy) or the like or to buy books to lend to poor scholars to study from, he may use the money for such purposes. In the case of books, he must be careful to inscribe in them that they are dedicated to public use so that his children may not acquire them by adverse possession.

6. If one gives to his grown sons and daughters . . . for whose support he is no longer responsible . . . or makes gifts to his father whom he cannot support otherwise than out of funds intended for *tzedaka*, all such contributions are deemed *tzedaka*. Nay, more, he must prefer such persons to others, a needy relative to the other poor of his city, the poor of his own city to those of another place, as it is said: "Your poor and needy brother in your land" (*Deuteronomy* 15:11). But the communal collectors (*gabbayim* of *tzedaka*) should be careful not to favor their own needy kin more than other poor folk.

7. Any person who gives *tzedaka* with a disagreeable countenance and downcast mien, . . . transgresses the command: ". . . your heart shall not be grieved when you give" (*Deuteronomy* 15:10). He must give, instead, with a pleasant countenance and with joy, and must express sympathy for the poor man in his trouble, as Job said: "If I have not wept for him that was in trouble and if my soul grieved not for the needy" (*Job* 30:25). He should speak words of consolation, as it is said: "And I caused the widow's heart to sing."

8. It is forbidden to turn back a poor man emptyhanded when he begs alms, even if one gives as little as a dried fig, as it is said: "Let not the oppressed turn back in confusion" (*Psalms* 74:21). If one has nothing at all to give one should cheer him with words. It is forbidden to rebuke a poor man or to raise one's voice and shout at him, for his heart is broken and crushed, as the Psalmist says: "A broken and contrite heart you will not despise." Woe unto him who puts a poor man

unto shame. One should be instead like a father to him both in compassion and in words, as it is said: "I was a father to the needy" (*Job* 29:16).

9. The highest degree of *tzedaka*, beyond all others, is to uphold a poor man before he is completely impoverished, to give him a substantial gift in a dignified manner to be used in earning a living, or to lend him a sum for that purpose, or to associate him in some venture or to procure for him some business or some work, in order to repair his fortunes so that he should not need help from others. That is meant by ". . . you shall uphold him . . ." (*Leviticus* 25:35), keep him so that he may not sink into utter destitution.

10. One should be careful to give the *tzedaka* as secretly as possible; and if it can be given in such a way that the donor does not know to whom he is giving and the recipient does not know from whom he is receiving, that is very good indeed.

11. One should always keep oneself far removed from taking *tzedaka*, and should suffer want rather than take assistance from others; for so commanded our Sages (their memory for a blessing): "Make thy Sabbath like a weekday, and do not require the help of others . . ." (*Sabbath* 118). Even an honored scholar who becomes impoverished should exercise some craft, even an undignified one, rather than to require help from others.

12. Whoever should accept help because he is unable to sustain himself without it, due to illness, physical disability or old age, and yet is too proud to accept; he is, indeed, a shedder of his own blood, and commits a mortal sin. He has for his suffering nothing but sin and transgression. Yet whoever puts off as long as possible the taking of *tzedaka* and suffers want, not out of pride, but rather in order not to burden the community, he will live to be a support of others. Regarding him Scripture says: "Blessed is the man that trusts in the Lord" (*Jeremiah* 17:7).

Index